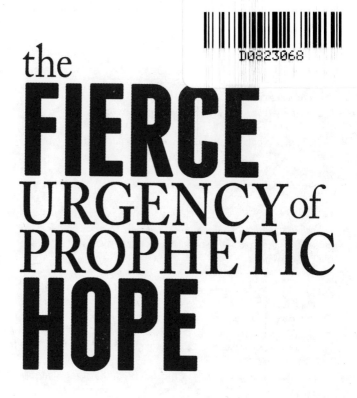

the
FIERCE
URGENCY of
PROPHETIC
HOPE

WENDELL L. GRIFFEN
PROLOGUE BY **WALTER BRUEGGEMANN**
FOREWORD BY **ALLAN AUBREY BOESAK**
AFTERWORD BY **EMILIE M. TOWNES**

JUDSON PRESS
PUBLISHERS SINCE 1824

Join our mailing list for updates and special offers.
www.judsonpress.com/mailing_list.cfm

The Fierce Urgency of Prophetic Hope
© 2017 by Wendell L. Griffen. All rights reserved.

Interior design by Wendy Ronga, Hampton Design Group.
Cover design by Danny Ellison.

Library of Congress Cataloging-in-Publication
Names: Griffen, Wendell L. (Pastor), author. Title: The fierce urgency of prophetic hope/Wendell L. Griffen; foreword by Allan Aubrey Boesak; afterword by Emilie M. Townes. Description: First [edition]. | Valley Forge: Judson Press, 2017. Identifiers: LCCN 2017001568 | ISBN 9780817017866 (pbk.: alk. paper) Subjects: LCSH: Sermons. Classification: LCC BV4253 .G75 2017 | DDC 252—dc23 LC record available at https://lccn.loc.gov/2017001568
Cataloging-in-Publication Data available upon request.
Contact cip@judsonpress.com.

Printed in the U.S.A.
First printing 2017.

Advance Praise

"With uncompromised boldness, Wendell Griffen reminds clergy and lay persons of God's call to prophetic witness and prophetic citizenship on the journey towards liberation and justice."

—Rev. Dr. Iva Carruthers, General Secretary,
Samuel DeWitt Proctor Conference

"To read this book is to be reminded of the biblical prophet/judge role of Samuel. Just as Samuel spoke against the abuse of power by the king of Israel, Griffen challenges twenty-first-century preachers to proclaim justice after the election of Donald Trump as US president."

—Marvin A. McMickle, PhD, President,
Colgate Rochester Crozer Divinity School

"Rev. Griffen's work is timely and prophetic."

—Reggie L. Williams, PhD, Assistant Professor of Christian Ethics,
McCormick Theological Seminary

"This judge, pastor, and law professor applies the wisdom of Hebrew prophets, Jesus, and liberation theology to white evangelical Christians' election of a populist who does not embody the Christian values they claim to stand for."

—Ray Higgins, PhD, Coordinator,
Cooperative Baptist Fellowship of Arkansas

"A gift for those who need courage to speak about politics and faith worthy of the human spirit. The work and witness of Wendell Griffen encourages justice-seekers in the public square."

—Forrest Harris, President, American Baptist College; Director,
Black Church Studies, Vanderbilt University Divinity School

"Reading this book kindles a renewed spirit in me for a justice-driven spirituality. I trust it will have the same impact for others."

—Molly T. Marshall, PhD, President and Professor of
Theology and Spiritual Formation, Central Baptist Theological Seminary

"Wendell Griffen challenges us to wield hope fiercely as an offensive weapon of our spiritual, political, and social struggle in incredibly tumultuous times. Pastoral leaders, small-group facilitators, and church school teachers will find this an invaluable resource."

—Rev. Aidsand F. Wright-Riggins III, DMin, Executive Director Emeritus,
ABHMS, Catalyst, Greater Philadelphia Network of Spiritual Progressives

In memory of my parents, Bennie L. and Josephine L. Griffen.
Their faithful lives introduced me to God's grace
and to the gospel of Jesus Christ.

Dedicated to my wife, Dr. Patricia L. Griffen, and
to our sons, Martyn and Elliott Griffen.
Years ago, for Father's Day,
they gave me an electric memory typewriter.
The gift's accompanying note read, "For your book."
So, this is the book, a belated present to them,
and the result of their hopeful encouragement.
I am thankful for their love,
and I pray that this product of their investment
honors the support they have given me.

Contents

Prologue

It is just right that Wendell Griffen should write a book on prophetic hope. When I think of Griffen I think of fierce urgency, for he has been fierce for a long time about a cluster of urgent issues. But prophetic utterance (of the kind he offers here) is never generic or in a vacuum. It is always triggered by a particular moment in the life of the world. Here Griffen's response is triggered by the 2016 election of Donald Trump as forty-fifth President of the United States. Behind that moment in history, however, is a mass of amorphous anxiety, a fearful awareness that the old certitudes are gone and the future is not yet known.

Thus Wendell Griffen responds in a way that recalls the lyrics of James Russell Lowell, "Once to every man and nation, comes the moment to decide, / In the strife of truth with falsehood, for the good or evil side; / Some great cause, some great decision, offering each the bloom or blight, / And the choice goes by forever, 'twixt that darkness and that light." Ours is just such a moment of making choices and choosing futures.

First, Griffen sees that we are in a moment of "moral and ethical dwarfism" when our sensibility to our neighbors and their issues has shriveled to indifference. As a result, our capacity to act in responsible and compassionate ways has nearly disappeared. The book is a bid that we recover moral courage and ethical awareness so that we may act in inconvenient ways that build neighborliness as the condition of our common well-being.

Second, by his shrewd exposition of the Zacchaeus narrative in Luke 19:1-10, Griffen sees the urgent need for conversion that demands repentance. Such repentance as conversion, moreover, is not a glib apology. Repentance has demanding ethical implications that require reparation. Thus the tax collector Zacchaeus not only repented of his fraudulent actions in response to Jesus but promised restitution as a cost of reconciliation. In the US today a similar, systemic practice of oppression and exploitation has long robbed many sectors of our society. When we recover from our moral dwarfism, we may notice the wounds caused in our history, and we may awaken to the imperative of significant systemic repentance.

Third, as I read the book I thought of Bonhoeffer's phrase "cheap grace," which in his moment of history was not a generic idea of relaxed faith. It related specifically to his historic context in which German Christians refused to choose between gospel and National Socialism. Or more properly they did not even recognize that they faced an either/or choice. So also in our moment, Griffen sees that we face a defining decision between embracing *gospel neighborliness* or accommodating to *systemic greed and anxiety* that are toxic to the point of death.

Fourth, Griffen is especially critical of "good evangelicals," a term he uses ironically to refer to those who are zealous, pious, and generally ethical, but who do not see the public implications of gospel neighborliness nor how failure to apply such gospel principles has resulted in a political economy that has lost its way. (As a card-carrying liberal I wish that Griffen had extended his critique to "good liberals," who talk better than we walk.)

Before he finishes, Griffen will take up the Song of Songs concerning sexuality. Who knew that in such a book appeal would be made to this erotic poetry and to its concern for well embraced sexuality that amounts to a caring celebration of the gifts of creation. But Griffen does that in a very fine read of the text.

In the end Griffen is about hope—not the hope of romantic optimism, nor the easy hope that passively assumes the future belongs only to God. Rather Griffen's prophetic hope is serious about a sustained, risky investment in a future willed by God. It is an insistence that a different social possibility can be imagined, chosen, and performed because the God of the gospel is not domesticated into old patterns of social injustice.

I am deeply grateful for Wendell's witness in this fierce statement that is both a faithful assurance and a prophetic summons to create a reconciling, emancipatory future.

—Walter Brueggemann
Columbia Theological Seminary

Foreword

In a slim but memorable and important volume, Dr. Marvin McMickle, president of Colgate Rochester Divinity School and strong prophetic preacher in his own right, asked a question that has become the title of his book: "Where have all the prophets gone?" It is a searing critique of the loss of the prophetic tradition in the church, as well as a deep yearning for that tradition to be reclaimed. Reading this book, one realizes with growing gratitude to God that at least one preacher has heard that cry and has responded with forceful prophetic preaching, sincere intellectual wrestling with the challenges of our day, and thoughtful thought-provoking engagement with the fearful, distressing times in which we live and are called to witness to God's compassionate justice, endless mercy, righteous judgment, life-giving hope, and inclusive love. Here, in the sermons and lectures of Wendell Griffen, we find it all.

The great German theologian Helmut Gollwitzer, like his friend and colleague Dietrich Bonhoeffer, was a prophet of the first hour of the Confessing Church fighting Hitler and the Nazification of the German Evangelical Church (and did me the unforgettable honor of writing a foreword for my first book of sermons to appear in German). Writing in 1980, in a preface to a book of his own sermons, Gollwitzer speaks a word as relevant today as it was then. He says preaching is a singular form of speech, developed from its earliest days by the Christian church to hand down the history of the great hope, the history of Israel and its God, the history of Jesus of Nazareth, and the history of the spiritual explosion of the Resurrection Community. But Gollwitzer is not just speaking of preaching in general. He is speaking of prophetic preaching, the kind of preaching that is burning on every single page of this book. That is why prophetic preaching is not a homiletical lullaby, it is a "spiritual explosion."

Those who commit themselves to this great tradition as a preacher, Gollwitzer writes, will discover "that in no other form of speech are things taken so seriously, is our whole existence so challenged, even put at risk. In no form of speech does our word itself so much take the form of action, of intervention in the history of the hearers, as in this."[1]

For every preacher, this must sound thoroughly intimidating, or hopelessly idealistic, perhaps because we have forgotten what we are doing when we stand in the pulpit to preach, or maybe it is just that we have come to take preaching so frighteningly lightly. "Most sermons these days," according to the late Paul Lehmann's critique, "are notably irrelevant." He writes, "Sermons—even carefully crafted ones—are nearly always event-less. They are a compound of either the obvious and the trivial, or the learned and the commonplace—or both—on the move from the latitudinous to the platitudinous. Everybody likes to hear what everybody knows—and effectively dismisses as not worth bothering about."[2] Not so with the sermons and lectures in this wonderful, challenging, inspiring book.

But the sermon, I discovered very early in my ministry, is an event in which the preacher gives something of herself away, making herself vulnerable. The preacher clothes himself, his convictions, his faith in the very defenselessness of the gospel itself. The preacher surrenders to the concreteness of the gospel because the gospel is about the concreteness of the life, death, and resurrection of Jesus of Nazareth, the concreteness of the life of God's people in the world, and the concreteness of the reign of God. That great history and hope, affirmed in and through what Johann Baptist Metz characterized as the "dangerous" or "subversive" memory of Christ,[3] puts one's very existence at risk. Helmut Gollwitzer chose for that great, subversive hope in that great, subversive history of the struggle for the freedom to belong to Jesus Christ, to stand where Christ stood—namely with the despised, the unchosen, and the persecuted, and against the chosen, the powerful, and those deemed worthy in Hitler's Germany. Wendell Griffen's writing and preaching invites that hope-filled reach toward Christ, to stand where Christ is always to be found.

The year 2016 made at least this crystal clear and absolutely undeniable. "Is this what a national nervous breakdown looks like?" asks journalist William Boardman of the post-election United States. But the malaise is much deeper and broader. In as many ways as we can count, ours is a world in murderous upheaval. Endless war is causing endless suffering and endless death for the sake of endless profits. The combined wealth of the world's richest one percent will have overtaken that of the other 99 percent by the end of 2016. One in nine people do not have enough to eat, and more than one billion people live on less than $1.25 a day.

The so-called economic recovery of the last few years was in essence only a recovery for the rich: the richest one percent have seen their share of the global wealth increase from 44 percent in 2009 to 48 percent in 2014, and it will climb to more than 50 percent in 2016. No doubt 2017 will see this distressing trend grow. In concrete terms, members of the global elite had an average wealth of $2.7 million per adult in 2014. In comparison 80 percent of the world's population had an average of a mere $3,851 per adult. In a time of economic crisis and calls for more austerity for the working classes, the wealth of the richest 80 percent doubled in cash terms between 2009 and 2014.

In the United States, the prison-industrial-capitalist complex has grown into an $86 billion business. A young person of color walking down the street is absolutely worthless to the wealthy and the powerful, as the spirits of Michael Brown, Sandra Bland, and the many, many others testify. Once in prison though, he or she becomes a capital-generating commodity of great worth. An inmate will generate between $30,000 to $40,000 per year in profits for the privatized prison system. Only when they can be turned into profits do they count.

All over the world, no less on my own continent of Africa, God's LGBTQ children are shamed, targeted, threatened, humiliated, and hunted down. Every imaginable and unimaginable indignity is heaped upon them. In countries like Uganda and Nigeria, they are criminalized and killed—all in the name of a terrifyingly homophobic Jesus. They are all crying out, "How long?" The preacher in this book has heard that cry and responded with hope and courage.

Just as Wendell Griffen does now, Helmut Gollwitzer saw the power of Hitler's words as they mesmerized a whole nation and captivated the church. Yet he saw how the power of the Word of God can challenge the power of evil when the words themselves become action, when we take the risks that Christ took for the sake of that salvific intervention in history. Gollwitzer discovered this because he was not afraid to follow the full consequences of his prophetic faithfulness in the struggle against Hitler. His preaching itself became a commitment to the struggle for justice, truth, and prophetic faithfulness, and in so doing, it became the faithful presence of the promises of God.

Preaching in what he called "a world shaken by deadly convulsions," Gollwitzer held fast to Christ, the center of his faith and the hope of the world, and this brought him to painful but righteous choices, struggle and sacrifice, and his discovery of the inseparability of faith and costly discipleship. It is the discovery I myself had made: when we say Jesus, we have to say justice. That is the heart of prophetic preaching seeking to be faithful to the promises of God.

While reading this book, I had the constant feeling of gratitude wash over me: the prophets have not all gone. Some of us may have gotten lost; we may have been cowed by the power of empire or lured by the temptations of empire. Some of us may not have been able, unlike the midwives of Exodus 1, to overcome our fear of the empire with our love for the Lord, our trust of the Lord, and our commitment to following Jesus. But not all of us have gone. Read this book and be convinced, convicted, and inspired.

—Rev. Dr. Allan Aubrey Boesak

Notes

1. Quoted in Dean G. Stroud, ed., *Preaching in Hitler's Shadow: Sermons of Resistance in the Third Reich* (Grand Rapids: William B. Eerdmans, 2013), 115.

2. Paul Lehmann,

3. See Johann Baptist Metz, "The Future in the Memory of Suffering," in *Faith and*

the Future, eds. Johann Baptist Metz and Jürgen Moltmann, trans. John Griffiths (Maryknoll, NY: Orbis Books, 1995), 7–8.

South African theologian Rev. Dr. Allan Aubrey Boesak is a humanitarian, social justice activist, author of numerous books and scholarly articles, and a leading authority on liberation theology. In June 2013, Christian Theological Seminary and Butler University named Dr. Boesak the Desmond Tutu Chair of Peace, Global Justice, and Reconciliation Studies, following his role as a theologian and visiting professor at both institutions during the 2012–13 academic year.

Acknowledgments

I owe thanks to many followers of Jesus for helping me understand and trust the liberating love of God. For the past seven years, the inclusive and progressive members known as New Millennium Church of Little Rock, Arkansas, have served as my unwavering support and faith community. Each Sunday, we gather in the sanctuary of another congregation, Lakeshore Drive Baptist Church, and affirm these words as our commitment to oneness and purpose:

> *We praise and worship God, together. We petition God, together. We proclaim God, together. We welcome all persons in God's love, together. We live for God, in every breath and heartbeat, as followers of Jesus Christ by the power of the Holy Spirit, together.*

I thank God for New Millennium Church, for our partnership with Lakeshore Drive Baptist Church, and for what the Holy Spirit has done and continues to do through our shared fellowship. The views expressed in this book come from the rich experiences gained with those congregations. I thank them for listening to my sermons, praying for me, caring for me, and prodding me to follow the divine impulse into deeper dimensions of grace, truth, justice, and hope. I especially thank New Millennium members Suzette Cannon, Rev. Demetria Edwards, Grif Stockley, and our encourager, Dr. Carol T. Mitchell of Omaha, Nebraska (who continues to request manuscript copies of my weekly sermons).

Rev. Dr. J. Alfred Smith Sr., pastor emeritus of Allen Temple Baptist Church in Oakland, California, is the ministerial elder in whom I have been most able to confide. The trajectory of that path began the afternoon I heard his voice on the church's answering machine when he praised my sermons he had read on the Ethics Daily website (www.ethicsdaily.com). Dr. Smith and his wife, Rev. Bernestine Smith, have faithfully prayed for me and our congregation, and he has often encouraged me to publish my thoughts in book form. He also introduced me to South African freedom fighter and theologian Dr. Allan Aubrey Boesak, his wife, Elna, and their daughter, Andrea, when they moved to the United States.

If Dr. Smith is my preaching mentor, and Dr. Boesak is my trusted theological influence, then Rev. Dr. Jeremiah A. Wright Jr., pastor emeritus of Trinity United Church of Christ in Chicago, and social justice icon Dr. Iva E. Carruthers, executive secretary of the Samuel DeWitt Proctor Conference, are the seasoned siblings and prophetic whetstones who have helped sharpen my vision about the radical and liberating grace of God. Drs. Smith, Boesak, Wright, and Carruthers have blessed my ministry, preached at New Millennium, befriended me, and been confidantes and mentors. I am deeply grateful to them, along with Dr. Frederick D. Haynes III, of Friendship West Baptist Church, and the other trustees of the Samuel DeWitt Proctor Conference, Inc. Working with them has blessed me with theological fellowship and pastoral encouragement, allowed me to benefit from their prophetic humor, and equipped me to better celebrate the divine adventure known as proclaiming the gospel of Jesus. I am grateful to Dr. Smith for introducing me into that esteemed circle. I extend additional recognition to Dr. Boesak for writing this book's Foreword, and for that special conversation we shared in a Dallas, Texas, hotel lobby—it forever changed how I think of myself as preacher.

A host of others, both pastors and parishioners, have impacted my theological walk and were kind to me at crucial points in my ministry—some through personal relationships and others through study and reading. The writings of black liberation scholar Dr. James H. Cone, along with the teachings of the great American deans of preaching, Rev. Drs. Gardner C. Taylor and Samuel DeWitt Proctor, have spoken to my frustrations with evangelical notions of what it means to follow Jesus. And Dr. Reggie Williams, professor of ethics at McCormick

Acknowledgments

Theological Seminary in Chicago and author of *Bonhoeffer's Black Jesus*,[1] also encouraged me to write and to consider circulating my work beyond the congregations I have been blessed to serve.

These people have made a difference in my life, much like the way Dr. Howard Thurman's life was transformed by a random act of kindness from a stranger who paid for his trunk expenses to Jacksonville from Daytona Beach, Florida, so he could attend high school.[2] The big difference has been that I have known the names of my benefactors and been stretched by their fellowship beyond a single encounter.

Other men and women of God have poured into me and have been especially influential in my spiritual formation: Rev. J. P. Story, Rev. H. R. Green, Rev. G. H. Jones, Mr. Hugh Simmons, Mrs. Odie B. Williams, Rev. A. G. Easter, Rev. C. H. Harris, Rev. A. William Terry, Rev. Robert Willingham, Mr. Samuel and Mrs. Mavis Posey, Mr. Acie and Mrs. Frances Johnson, Deacons B. L. and Richard Torrence and Mrs. Mary Torrence, Dr. W. T. Keaton, Rev. Geroy G. Osborne, Rev. C. Dennis Edwards, Dr. Robert U. Ferguson, Rev. Howard "Flash" Gordon, Rev. Stephen Copley, Rabbi Emeritus Eugene Levy, Dr. Ray Higgins, Dr. William D. Lindsey, Dr. Raouf Halaby, Dr. Isaac Mwase, Rev. Dr. Samuel Berry McKinney, and Rev. Dr. William J. Shaw.

Since New Millennium Church was organized, I've shared my weekly sermons and writings via the Internet. I want to thank those who logged in, signed on and listened to, and accepted what I proclaimed.

Finally, I must express appreciation to Dr. Smith and to Rev. Dr. Aidsand Wright-Riggins III, executive director emeritus of American Baptist Home Mission Societies (ABHMS). They are responsible for bringing me to the attention of Laura Alden, publisher of Judson Press, and Rev. Rebecca Irwin-Diehl, editor of Judson. Thank you, Laura and Rebecca, for considering my thoughts and helping me become the writer my wife, sons, beloved congregation members, and ministry colleagues believe I am and can be.

—Wendell L. Griffen

Notes

1. Reggie L. Williams, *Bonhoeffer's Black Jesus: Harlem Renaissance Theology and an Ethic of Resistance* (Waco: Baylor University Press, 2014).

2. See Howard Thurman, *With Head and Heart* (New York, NY: Harcourt Brace and Company, 1979), 24–25. Thurman dedicated his autobiography as follows: "To the stranger in the railroad station in Daytona Beach who restored my broken dream sixty-five years ago."

Introduction

The Fierce Urgency of Prophetic Hope is my attempt to help follow-ers of Jesus—those social-justice-minded pastors, congregational leaders, religious educators, grassroots activists and advocates, and other faithful persons—to ponder one question: *How are we to be committed to the cause of Jesus during and after the presidency of Donald J. Trump?* For those of us who are committed to do justice and love mercy, President Trump's election was more than an elec-toral surprise. It was a distressing moral and ethical reality that forces us to ponder how President Trump's political support by peo-ple who self-identify as evangelical followers of Jesus can be recon-ciled with the love and justice imperatives of the religion of Jesus. In many ways *The Fierce Urgency of Prophetic Hope* will examine the religious contributors to the current divisive mood within the coun-try—a mood defined by white racism, patriarchy and misogyny, crass materialism, militarism, imperialism, white religious national-ism, and xenophobia.

Dr. Martin Luther King Jr. once asked, "Where do we go from here?" The answer is: *prophetic hope.*

I believe in a subversive and liberating vision of hope based on the faith tradition inspired by the religion of Jesus. Acting on that hope allows those who believe in the Spirit of God to confront, condemn, and overcome political, social, commercial, and religious actions that promote alienation, fear, hate, and despair.

That means I believe we can survive distressing seasons. There are, however, questions to be asked and answered, such as:

■ How can people inspired by the gospel of Jesus rethink the ways we understand God (theology), interpret Scripture (hermeneutics), and behave (ethics) as prophetic followers of Jesus Christ?

■ What does it mean to be a "prophetic follower of Jesus"? Will we obey lessons found in Scripture and across human history that show what being "prophetic" involves? What will that obedience mean for how we live?

■ How can we be prophetic followers and remain hopeful and faithful in the face of a presidency that appears determined to roll back cherished freedoms and hard-won civil rights? To borrow from Dr. Boesak, "Dare we speak of hope?" How will we behave as hopeful and prophetic followers of Jesus?

Throughout this volume, readers will notice I use the terms *followers of Jesus, the religion of Jesus,* or *disciples of Jesus,* rather than *Christians.* I do so because Christianity, as a world religion, is often identified with, and considered complicit in, imperialism, colonialism, oppressive capitalism, white supremacy, racism, sexism, homophobia, militarism, environmental injustice, xenophobia, and a host of other "isms." The 2016 presidential election, due in substantial part to votes President Trump received from people who self-identified as "evangelical Christian conservatives," proves the point. Following the example of Howard Thurman, I do not associate following Jesus and will not have my religious identity associated with those obvious violations of the divine command that we love others as we love ourselves.

Let me offer some thoughts on how I hope this book will be read, understood, and used. First, I wrote *The Fierce Urgency of Prophetic Hope* for people who believe that the life and ministry of Jesus, as chronicled in the New Testament, is the most authoritative evidence on how the power of God is intended to work in and for individuals and communities across creation. And I am writing for people who are considering joining the circle of those who believe in Jesus Christ.

Those reasons do not make my book useless to people who do not believe in God or do not see the weight and relevance of the Holy Bible. I hope people who have not found the importance of faith, religion, or God will be curious enough to read the book. I pray my words will somehow help transform their lives.

Much of what I have written has been uttered from New Millennium's pulpit. The first and the four concluding chapters are modifications and adaptations of sermons delivered to our congregation. Other chapters are lectures about issues of social injustice that I consider especially troubling to people who believe in the love of God, justice, and mercy.

Readers will quickly conclude that I do not consider support for the presidency of Donald Trump to be in keeping with the redemptive love of God manifested by the life, ministry, death, resurrection, and lordship of Jesus Christ. But readers will also find that I am equally moved to criticize Presidents Barack Obama and Bill Clinton, Secretary Hillary Clinton, and any other public official whose views and conduct violate the biblical command to love God with his or her entire being, to care for the most vulnerable, and to treat our neighbors as ourselves.

My sense of justice is inspired by the gospel of Jesus Christ and the Hebrew prophets of old. I am not driven by notions of political partisanship or professional affinity. My understanding of the gospel and the prophetic tradition is that God deserves my ultimate allegiance. I do not owe equal or higher fidelity to nations, rulers, political parties, or any other aspirants to power.

I urge those who read these pages to treat my comments as just that—my thoughts and opinions on the national and global consequences of the contentious and highly controversial 2016 presidential election that will impact the intersection of politics and faith in the marketplace of ideas. As the apostle Paul wrote, none of us sees or understands anything as clearly as God does. Rather, "Now we see in a mirror, dimly . . . Now, I know only in part . . ." (1 Corinthians 13:12). Please consider my words as admittedly dim and partial, imperfect and therefore questionable notions about God, the religion of Jesus, salvation, and social justice.

I pray readers will find this book useful for personal reflection, group study discussions, ministry formation, and guidance. That said, I predict the book will contain some omissions or something with which readers might disagree. I, alone, bear that responsibility. If any good comes from this endeavor, the Spirit of God deserves the credit. And if I have caused harm or offense, I pray that readers and the Holy Spirit will forgive me.

Finally, I am a follower of Jesus the Christ. I am blessed to be called *husband, dad, brother, judge, pastor, kinsman,* and *friend* by the people I love and dearly cherish. I have received more than I could possibly imagine growing up in southwest Arkansas during the final days of Jim Crow segregation. The nurture and instruction I've received from those who follow Jesus helped shape my worldview. I will never be able to express how much their love, encouragement, fellowship, and trust have meant to me. I can only repeat what my father, Bennie Lee Griffen, would say: "Thank you, until you're better paid."

CHAPTER 1

Wisdom for Prophetic People in a Distressing Time[1]

This will give you an opportunity to testify. So make up your minds not to prepare your defense in advance; for I will give you words and a wisdom that none of your opponents will be able to withstand or contradict. You will be betrayed even by parents and brothers, by relatives and friends; and they will put some of you to death. You will be hated by all because of my name. But not a hair of your head will perish. By your endurance you will gain your souls. —Luke 21:13-19

We are living in distressing times.

The Sunday after the last presidential election, disciples of Jesus who believe that obedience to the gospel of Christ requires commitment to social justice sat stunned in worship houses throughout the country. It was the first Lord's Day after the November 8, 2016 election of President Donald J. Trump and Vice President Michael Richard Pence. Five days earlier, few people believed their win was a likely result, not even the political elite or Washington, DC insiders. Polling predictions leaned toward Secretary Hillary R. Clinton, and television anchors prior to election day treated her triumph as a foregone conclusion. But *they* were wrong. And prophetic followers of Jesus were plainly shocked.

Now, some questions must be answered. These include: What are prophetic followers of Jesus to do? How should we respond? Since the election, news outlets, in-depth magazine reports, even Facebook and YouTube postings have detailed a surge in acts of hate speech, as well as physical and online acts of racism. According to a detailed Southern Poverty Law Center report conducted after the election, women, immigrants, members of the LGBTQ community, blacks, Jews, persons perceived to be Muslims, and other groups have been subjected to harassment. Property has been defaced with hateful slurs. Trump's election led to protests in cities across the United States attended by people worried about how his unusual political ascension will affect peace, impact equality, and the affect health, safety, and sense of belonging for vulnerable and marginalized people.

We are living in a distressing time.

November 13, 2016—the Sunday after Donald J. Trump was elected the 45th president of the United States—was also one day after a mistrial was declared concerning the prosecution of Ray Tensing, a white former University of Cincinnati police officer who shot to death in 2015 an unarmed black motorist named Samuel DuBose.[2] A jury of ten white and two black persons was unable to agree whether Tensing murdered DuBose, despite having viewed the graphic body camera video showing Tensing aiming his service weapon directly into DuBose's vehicle.

So, on that Lord's Day, there were many distressing things, many disappointed people—a hung jury, a mistrial, a newly elected president who incited some fears—all the latest proof that black lives do not matter when it comes to law enforcement and other public and social policies in the United States.

We are living in a distressing time.

The tyranny of white supremacy that set up, operated, and profited from racial segregation in public education before the US Supreme Court declared it unconstitutional in the 1954 *Brown v. Board of Education* landmark decision[3] in Little Rock, Arkansas—where I live—and elsewhere is disguised as support for school choice, charter schools, and school vouchers. The charter school movement to privatize and commodify public education is merely segregation by another name, no matter what politicians and so-called education reformers would have people believe. As activist Anne Zerrien-Lee observed,

"Our public education system has been targeted by corporate bandits that are increasingly successful at siphoning off education funding for their own profit. They are in fact destroying public education in order to grab the tax dollars that support it."[4]

We are living in a distressing time for people who care about social justice. We are living in a distressing time for people who care about democracy. We are living in a distressing time for people who care about women and girls; for people who are black or brown; for those who are immigrants, lesbian, gay, bisexual, transgender, disabled, or frail from sickness; for people who are followers of Islam; and for people who are vulnerable and marginalized. We are living in a distressing time for people who seek peace and desire to live as people of inclusive community.

So, what can prophetic people learn from Jesus of Nazareth about how to behave in this distressing time? .

The setting for the biblical lesson from Luke's Gospel is full of political drama. It took place in Jerusalem, the capital city of Judea, where Jesus would be arrested for insurrection against the Roman government based on falsified evidence. Enemies within the religious establishment would call for his death. Pontius Pilate, the Roman governor, would condemn Jesus to be crucified despite knowing his innocence.

So, when Jesus heard people speaking about the beautiful temple in Jerusalem, with its ornate stones and other prized objects, and predicted it would be demolished at a future time, some who heard his words were distressed. They wanted to know when to expect the ominous event, and what would be its threatening signs: "Teacher, when will this be, and what will be the sign that this is about to take place?" (Luke 21:7). People with good sense want to know the warning signs for oncoming negative conditions and trouble. Most of us want weather alerts that warn us when storms are over the horizon or blizzards are coming. We want to know the warning symptoms for life-threatening illnesses. We want warning signs—signals. We want a heads-up. And we want to know how to interpret those signs when we receive them. We want to know what *tornado watch* means. We want to know how to process the meaning of *flash flood warnings*.

The people who heard Jesus predict that the Jerusalem temple would be destroyed wanted to know what events and actions would signal such a threat to the cultural and religious heritage of the Jewish people. They were thinking about the loss of their most cherished religious landmark. They heard Jesus speak about it being demolished at some future time. They were desperate to know the indicators for such a cataclysmic event. And who could blame them?

The people who heard Jesus speak on the temple's eventual destruction were not thinking about the end of the world. Let me say that again in case you missed it. *They were not thinking about the end of the world.* They were thinking about the loss of their religious, cultural, and political landmark. Their thoughts were on losing a religious edifice that King Herod started rebuilding nineteen years before Jesus was born. That rebuilding project more than doubled the size of the temple mount. While work on the temple took eighteen months, work on the outer courts where people gathered for speeches and healings (see Acts 3:11; 5:12) would continue throughout the lifetime of Jesus until 62–64 CE.

But less than ten years after the effort to rebuild the Herodian temple was completed, the Romans destroyed it in 70 CE. The Romans plundered its ornate furnishings and hauled them to Rome. The Romans visually portrayed the siege and burning of Jerusalem in large paintings that were paraded on wagons in a triumphal procession to Rome in 71 CE.[5] When Jerusalem and its temple were destroyed in 70 CE, followers of Jesus thought that event confirmed what he predicted many years earlier.

I suspect more than a few folks might be surprised to learn this passage is not about the end of the world. It has been often preached, studied, and taught from that point of view. That's probably because every generation somehow figures its time marks the end of history. The pop music genius known as Prince famously set that thinking to music in his song *1999,* about the end of the twentieth century.[6] He wrote about and sang about partying until the end of time and the lights go out. As someone accurately put it, only a genius like Prince could drop protest thoughts about the constant threat of war into a dance song. My point—and I think what Jesus emphasized—is that we tend to view threats to political, cultural, and religious icons as omens of the apocalypse, the end of time. But Jesus warned us not to do so in these words: "Beware that you are not led astray; for many will come in my name and say, 'I am he!' and, 'The time is near!' Do not go after them" (Luke 21:8).

In other words, don't get twisted out of shape when threats to our political, cultural, and religious structures happen and folks arrive claiming, in God's name, to be some version of Jesus.

■ Don't get bent out of shape when President Trump or another politician or religious personality claims to be the savior the world needs.

■ Don't run around like the fabled Chicken Little who shouted, "The sky is falling! The sky is falling," because Ray Tensing wasn't found guilty of murdering Samuel DuBose, despite the evidence and the body camera video showing he shot DuBose in the head.

■ Don't think the world is coming to an end because white supremacists and corporate opportunists are determined to cannibalize public education for private profit to the detriment of public school students, and especially children from marginalized and historically mistreated communities.

Yes, this stuff is distressing. But that doesn't mean the world is about to end. Yes, it appears that President Trump is a remarkably misguided and unfair leader. Yes, he claims to be the answer to everything from income inequality to immigration struggles. Yes, he bragged he could sexually assault women because of his maleness, wealth, and celebrity. None of those things, though, mean the world is about to end. They merely mean voters elected someone who appears to be a remarkably ill-prepared and unjust president, however distressing that may be to followers of Jesus who care about love and justice.

Jesus predicted that there would be reports of "wars and insurrections" before the great temple Herod expanded was demolished

5

(Luke 21:9). He warned that there would be natural disasters, "great earthquakes, and in various places famines and plagues; there will be dreadful portents and great signs from heaven" (Luke 21:10-11). But in verse 9, Jesus said that before all those things happened, his followers would be targeted for persecution: "But before all this occurs, they will arrest you and persecute you; they will hand you over to synagogues and prisons, and you will be brought before kings and governors because of my name." Jesus warned his followers those events would happen before the temple was demolished. Those events were not to be considered omens for the end of time.

So, what was Jesus doing?

In Luke 21:13 we read these words from Jesus to his followers: "This will give you an opportunity to testify."

According to Jesus, this distressing season will provide opportunities for prophetic people to challenge, confront, and condemn unjust practices, policies, and systems. This distressing time will give us opportunities to act with prophetic courage and live with prophetic hope.

Mid-1980s hip-hop star M.C. Hammer often used the expression "Hammer Time" as his call to break into his famous dance routine. The distressing events Jesus predicted were not to be considered reasons for his followers to hide and be fearful. Jesus said they would be opportunities for moral witness about God's love and justice. Jesus was warning about things that would challenge his followers to be vigilant and courageous witnesses in the face of the distressing events he predicted they would experience.

I do not have M.C. Hammer's gift of movement or his clarion call to dance. But I do have the divine witness to declare. It is prophetic witness time.

I recently received an email message from Rev. Gilbert Caldwell, an eighty-three-year-old United Methodist champion for justice whom I met in April 2016 when New Millennium Church hosted a conference on affirming and embracing LGBTQ persons in the black church. Rev. Caldwell included me in an email posting he sent about a blog titled "White Christians Who Voted for Donald Trump: Fix This. Now" by

John Pavlovitz. Pavlovitz, who is on the pastoral staff of a white, non-denominational, evangelical church in Raleigh, North Carolina, wrote how students of color, women, Muslims, Latino students, and persons who appeared to be gay were targeted for abuse and mistreatment the day after Donald Trump was elected president of the United States. On November 9, 2016, the day after Donald Trump's electoral victory, Pavlovitz declared:

> This is the personal Hell we've unleashed . . . And if you're a white Christian and you voted for Donald Trump: You need to fix this. *Now*. . . . You need to do some knee to the dirt exploratory surgery with your Maker and figure out how you're going to respond to this—and then respond. For the love of God and for the love of the people you claim that God so loves—fix this. Now.[7]

Yes, it appears that President Trump and his administration will be insensitive, if not hateful, toward women, racial minorities, and people who are lesbian, gay, bisexual, and transgender. Yes, it seems they will disregard people with disabilities and mistreat immigrants, Muslims, and faithful people who resist oppression. And yes, white people who profess to be followers of Jesus flocked to vote for him. But none of those things mean the world is going to end. It means that followers of Jesus must be vigilant and prophetic witnesses for God's love and justice.

The criminal justice system has historically not been fair or equal to people of color and white people who are poor. The system appears to sanction abusive and homicidal behavior by people in law enforcement. That isn't proof the world is about end. It does, though, provide opportunities for followers of Jesus to engage in prophetic hope and citizenship for love and justice.

Public education is under attack from white supremacists, free market capitalists, and subservient lackeys of color. That doesn't mean the world is about to end. It means we have opportunities to be prophets of protest who are unafraid to challenge the forces of power. It means

7

we can be a people who will not flinch or cower in the face of racism and homophobic and xenophobic bigotry.

We are living in a distressing season.
We are living in distressing times.
But we have hope.
We are prophets of protest.
Now—let's get to it!

Discussion and Reflection Questions

1. Which social justice situations, practices, and issues are examples of distressing times for your community?

2. How have you personally responded to those distressing situations and events? How have other followers of Jesus responded?

3. If you are unable to identify personal or collective responses by followers of Jesus to distressing social justice situations in your community, who are the national "salt and light" voices, faces, and actors for social justice concerning those distressing situations?

Notes

1. This is a modified and adapted version of the sermon I preached during worship at New Millennium Church on November 13, 2016, the first Lord's Day after the November 8, 2016 election of Donald Trump to become the 45th President of the United States.

2. See www.nytimes.com/2016/11/13/us/ray-tensing-samuel-dubose-trial-deadlock.html?hpandaction=clickandpgtype=Home, accessed January 9, 2017.

3. 347 U.S. 483 (1954).

4. Anne Zerrien-Lee, "Who is Behind the Privatization of Public Education?" in *Pedagogy, Policy, and the Privatized City*, by Kristen L. Buras, Jim Randels, Kalamu Ya Salaam, and Students at the Center (New York: Teachers College Press, 2010), 126.

5. See Josephus, *The Jewish Wars* 7, 3–5.

6. See www.metrolyrics.com/1999-lyrics-prince.html, accessed January 9, 2017.

7. See johnpavlovitz.com/2016/11/10/white-christians-who-voted-for-donald-trump-fix-this-now//, accessed January 9, 2017.

CHAPTER 2

A Prophetic Perspective on the Rise of Donald Trump and American Empire[1]

He said to me: O mortal, stand up on your feet, and I will speak with you. And when he spoke to me, a spirit entered into me and set me on my feet; and I heard him speaking to me. He said to me, Mortal, I am sending you to the people of Israel, to a nation of rebels who have rebelled against me; they and their ancestors have transgressed against me to this very day. The descendants are impudent and stubborn. I am sending you to them, and you shall say to them, 'Thus says the Lord GOD.' Whether they hear or refuse to hear (for they are a rebellious house), they shall know that there has been a prophet among them. —Ezekiel 2:1-5

The voters' decision to elect Donald J. Trump as president of the United States forces prophetic followers of Jesus to confront, confess, and proclaim some inconvenient and unavoidable truths.

The Trump presidency was cheered, supported, and selected by a voting bloc who self-identify as evangelical Christian conservatives. While neurosurgeon Benjamin S. Carson (at print Dr. Carson was slated to be Secretary of Housing and Urban Development but had not been approved by Congress) showed that people of color can sell their moral and political birthrights for a chance to manipulate the levers of government, 92 percent of black voters did not support President Trump.[2] White Christian evangelicals—whom I consider to be white Christian nationalists—voted for Trump in overwhelming numbers and, by and large, elected him to the presidency.[3]

White evangelicals, who are offended by being identified as white nationalists, pretend they do not know that the voting history of "good" white Christian evangelicals is functionally the same as white supremacists, such as David Duke and Thom Robb, people who also claim to be followers of Jesus. Despite their shared voting history, "good" white Christian evangelicals believe themselves politically different from people like Duke, Robb, and Stephen K. Bannon, the president's Chief Strategist—whom many people consider to be clear examples of bigotry.

However, others understand that white Christian evangelicals and white Christian supremacists traditionally vote the same way.[4] Those self-proclaimed white evangelical Christians overwhelmingly voted for the president in 2016, knowing they were supporting the exact candidate endorsed by the Ku Klux Klan and Duke. And in so doing, their ballots were reminders of how their constituency voted in 1980 to end the presidency of Jimmy Carter.

President Carter, a white Southern Baptist Sunday school teacher, was committed to racial justice, gender equality, human rights, fairness for Palestinians, environmental protection, and worker justice. His personal and political record was clearly different from his rival, former California governor Ronald W. Reagan, who was embraced and championed by evangelical leaders like Jerry Falwell, Pat Robertson, Bill Bright (founder of Campus Crusade for Christ), and James Robison (who mentored a young Mike Huckabee, former governor of Arkansas).[5] White revivalists looked past Reagan's ecumenicalism and marital history in 1980—the same way "good" white evangelical Christians looked past President Trump's marital history and misogyny during the 2016 campaign—and elected Reagan as president because his positions on abortion, affirmative action, welfare, and militarism agreed with their sense of patriarchy, religious nationalism, imperialism, and white supremacy.

In the 2016 presidential election, Christian evangelicals supported Donald Trump, described in one BBC news article as "a thrice married casino-building businessman," over Secretary Hillary Clinton, a life-long United Methodist, former Sunday school teacher, and weekly prayer meeting attendee. One commentator wrote that Trump's campaign promise to nominate so-called "pro-life" candidates to the US Supreme Court was a major factor in the strong support he received from white evangelicals.[6]

Whenever I hear "good" evangelical followers of Jesus claim to be prophetic and insist they should not be viewed the same way as white Christian nationalists, I recall how Abraham and Sarah, the "good" exemplars of faith about whom we read in Genesis, mistreated Hagar and Ishmael. Abraham allowed Sarah to mistreat Hagar so badly during Hagar's pregnancy with Ishmael that Hagar ran away (Genesis 16:6). Hagar returned, but was thrown out of Abraham's household years later.

Sarah insisted that Abraham put Hagar, a single mother, and her teenaged son, Ishmael, out of his house and away from his protection and care as if they were garbage. So Abraham forced Hagar—his second wife and mother of his first son—to leave his protection (Genesis 21:14). The "good" Abraham didn't even give Hagar and Ishmael a beast to ride or carry their belongings. In this sense, Abraham and Sarah might be considered biblical predecessors of "good" evangelicals.

I also think about the "good" evangelical followers of Jesus when I reflect on Tamar, described in 2 Samuel 13:1 as "a beautiful sister" of David's son, Absalom. Tamar was raped by Amnon, David's oldest son (and her half-brother), who was the crown prince and a sexual predator. After Tamar was raped, she took shelter in Absalom's house but received neither justice nor vindication. Absalom told her to be silent about the crime she had suffered.

Meanwhile, King David (her father and the person who sent Tamar to Amnon's house, where she was raped) refused to punish Amnon "because he loved him, for he was his firstborn" (2 Samuel 13:21). David refused to prosecute and punish Amnon for raping his own daughter because Amnon was the crown prince. Likewise, "good" evangelical followers of Jesus consistently refuse to hold abusive and homicidal law enforcement officers accountable for terrorizing, beating, and slaying unarmed poor, black, brown, and white people.

11

In 2 Samuel 11, in the account of David and Bathsheba (the married woman whom David seduced while her husband, Uriah—one of David's soldiers—was at battle and later arranged to have him killed), David was eventually confronted and challenged by Nathan, the prophet. But no prophet showed up to confront David on Tamar's behalf about how David shielded a rapist from justice. Nathan didn't show up to confront David about his inaction after Amnon raped Tamar. Self-proclaimed "good" evangelicals remind me of Absalom, David, and Nathan. Women and girls have long been forsaken by "good" evangelicals, but they have not been alone.

"Good" evangelicals refused to support the 1963 March on Washington. "Good" evangelicals refused to support Dr. King's desegregation efforts in Birmingham, thereby triggering King's historic *Letter from Birmingham City Jail*. "Good" evangelicals didn't support Dr. King's call for the United States to end its military adventure in Southeast Asia. "Good" evangelicals didn't oppose the apartheid regime in South Africa.

"Good" evangelicals didn't support the war on poverty. "Good" evangelicals backed the "war on drugs" that is responsible for mass incarceration. "Good" evangelicals questioned the fairness of affirmative action remedies for the descendants of African slaves but did not protest when white workers were given preferential treatment for Federal Housing Administration (FHA) guaranteed loans. "Good" evangelicals didn't support reproductive freedom for women and girls. "Good" evangelicals didn't support the Equal Rights Amendment.

"Good" evangelicals didn't support Anita Hill during the confirmation hearings for then Judge Clarence Thomas. "Good" evangelicals haven't supported LGBTQ equality. "Good" evangelicals haven't supported justice for Palestinians. "Good" evangelicals haven't embraced the Black Lives Matter movement. "Good" evangelicals didn't oppose the war in Iraq.

"Good" evangelicals didn't oppose profiling of persons perceived to be Muslims or South Asians after the September 11, 2001 terrorist attacks on New York City and the Pentagon. They haven't supported

Planned Parenthood. They didn't support passage of the Affordable Care Act and aren't protesting plans to repeal it.

"Good" evangelicals remind me of Abraham, David, Absalom, and Nathan. They know that people are suffering because of oppressive policies, practices, and systems that violate the love ethic of Jesus. But, like the priest and Levite in the Good Samaritan lesson and like Abraham, Absalom, David, and Nathan, "good" evangelicals have consistently managed *not* to use their power, privilege, and moral authority to protect women, persons of color, immigrants, persons marginalized by the criminal punishment system, persons who are poor, LGBTQ persons, religious minorities, and others who are oppressed. Like "good" Abraham was of no help to Hagar and "good" David, Absalom, and Nathan were of no help to Tamar, "good" evangelical followers of Jesus have too often been no help to children of God oppressed by systemic injustices. The 2016 presidential election is merely the most recent example of that longstanding moral and ethical dwarfism.

The "good" evangelicals who place so much emphasis on knowing Scripture somehow have not benefited in their moral and ethical outlook from the examples of Shiphrah and Puah, the midwives in Egypt who engaged in civil disobedience and refused to obey a royal order that they kill male Hebrew babies at birth (see Exodus 1:15-21). "Good" evangelicals facing demands from xenophobic lawmakers about withdrawing public support for "sanctuary cities" might open their Bibles to Joshua and re-examine how a prostitute named Rahab defied a governmental order to hand over two undocumented immigrants (see Joshua 2). One wonders whether "good" evangelical followers of Jesus who profess commitment to religious liberty will draw on the example of Rahab in the face of calls by policymakers to round up and deport undocumented immigrants living in the United States. Given that so many "good" evangelical women followers of Jesus apparently supported a candidate who espoused such a policy during the 2016 presidential contest, it is apparent that the prophetic citizenship of Shiphrah, Puah, and Rahab is lacking among them or their "good" male evangelical colleagues.

One wonders if "good" evangelicals know this to be the case. One wonders if "good" evangelicals are concerned about their moral and ethical dwarfism. And one wonders if "good" evangelicals realize that the disconnect between their professed reverence for Scripture and their disregard for justice has caused many people to forsake organized religion.

According to a September 2016 survey by the Public Religion Research Institute (PRRI), one in four adults in the United States is not affiliated with any religion. That group is called the "nones" and is larger than any religious denomination. The survey shows that the number of unaffiliated young people has jumped from 10 percent in 1986 to 39 percent in 2016, a 400 percent increase.[7]

The hard truth evidenced by this survey report is that the gospel of Jesus is not about attendance, buildings, and cash (what someone has succinctly termed as the ABCs of church vitality). The gospel of Jesus is about being agents of God's grace, truth, peace, justice, mercy, and hope so that people and the creation are delivered from oppressive forces and conditions. That potential exists whenever people who embody the grace, truth, peace, justice, mercy, and hope of God show up, listen up, speak up, act up, and otherwise live as God's servants—prophetic citizens—in a suffering and despairing world. That potential exists whenever we see, hear, and respond in loving affirmation and with deeds of liberating justice when people are oppressed. This reality has yet to be understood and lived by "good" evangelical followers of Jesus.

"Good" white evangelicals and white supremacists like Duke, Robb, and other white nationalists who claim to be followers of Jesus have supported the same race-baiting, patriarchal, militaristic, imperialistic, homophobic, sexist, materialistic, and xenophobic candidates for two generations—since President Lyndon B. Johnson pushed through the Civil Rights Act of 1964, the Voting Rights Act of 1965, and the Fair Housing Act of 1968. President Trump's personal and commercial racism, white male supremacy and patriarchy, racist and misogynist bigotry, xenophobia, and pathological penchant for violence, oppressiveness, and fear of others will shape US policy for one reason: because "good" white evangelical Christians and white supremacists—white Christian nationalists—embraced his candidacy and elected him.

Therefore, white Christian nationalists—the Christian evangelicals and Christian supremacists—will be the US voters viewed as morally and ethically accountable for what happens during Trump's presidency, including the injustices, injuries, and other wrongs that may occur during his tenure. As is always the case in an American election, the nation has been urged by politicians to unify and heal wounds and fractures that were made, exposed, and worsened by Trump's candidacy and subsequent election. Followers of Jesus must consider those calls for unity and reconciliation with prophetic skepticism if they hope to be radical agents of the liberating gospel of Jesus Christ.

Allan A. Boesak and Curtiss Paul DeYoung have written that injustice must be challenged and severed at the roots to achieve a biblical reconciliation that produces a viable and sustained justice. Otherwise, people will continue to seek and reach for political accommodations. According to Boesak and DeYoung, those political arrangements invariably favor the rich and powerful and work to deny justice and dignity for people who are powerless. Meanwhile, more often than not, they falsely appear to respond to the needs for genuine healing by using language that sounds truthful but is actually deceitful. Boesak and DeYoung have termed those political accommodations *political pietism*. Boesak and DeYoung also caution that radical reconciliation often does not happen because of concerns for self-protection, out of fear, or because of a desire for acceptance by the governing powers, with the result that people become complicit in deceitful resolution, deny the demands of the gospel, and refuse solidarity with the powerless and oppressed. They have termed this result *Christian quietism*.[8]

To be prophetic, one must speak inconvenient and uncomfortable truth and dare to defy people in power. The Hebrew midwives Shiphrah and Puah defied Pharaoh's edict to kill Hebrew male babies. Moses did not collaborate with the Egyptian oppressors of the Hebrew people. The prophets and judges of old, such as Samuel, Nathan,

Deborah, Huldah, Elijah, Elisha, as well as the prophets whose ministries challenged and displeased rulers during the eighth century BCE, confronted, confounded, and condemned oppressive rulers and regimes. John the Baptist and Jesus rejected calls for religious-based nationalism that claimed to be superior to allegiance to divine love, justice, and truth. Followers of Jesus should bear these things in mind as the country is urged to "get over it," "fall in line," and be compliant with and complicit in policies, programs, and practices of the newly elected Trump presidency that are unjust.

Political pietism and Christian quietism will cause many people to fall in line with the usual post-election rhetoric about the need for people who hold varying views to find a way to work with the Trump administration. In the days that followed Trump's surprising victory, public appeals were made by people of various creeds to unify the nation from what a *New York Times* article called "a historically ugly presidential campaign."[9]

However, President Trump named Stephen Bannon as his White House chief strategist and senior counselor, the role performed by Valerie Jarrett in the Obama administration and by Karl Rove during the George W. Bush administration. Bannon is publicly known as having led *Breitbart News Network*, parent company of the far-right *Breitbart News* website, a favorite social media platform for white supremacist views. The "alt-right constituency, contemporary version of traditionalist racist organizations, is known for spouting bigoted, homophobic, sexist, anti-Semitic, and anti-Muslim rhetoric," according to a *New York Times* column.[10]

US Senator Jeff Sessions (R-AL), perhaps the first congressional member to call for building a wall along the country's southern borders to stem illegal immigration, was named Attorney General designee by Mr. Trump. During Reagan's presidency, Senator Sessions's nomination for a federal judgeship was defeated because of evidence he was hostile towards voting and civil rights efforts.[11] If Sessions's nomination is confirmed, he will oversee the Justice Department efforts on civil rights, human liberties for prisoners, and protection for the disabled, disenfranchised, and otherwise vulnerable.

At one point, former New York City mayor Rudolph Giuliani was a leading contender for Secretary of State, but he bowed out of the running before Mr. Trump selected Exxon Mobil CEO Rex Wayne Tillerson for that post.[12] Mayor Giuliani supported the controversial "stop and frisk" policing methods and policies that have been condemned as abusive toward the civil rights of persons of color.[13]

I belong to a congregation affiliated with the Cooperative Baptist Fellowship. Like the Southern Baptist Convention from which they broke only a quarter century ago, Cooperative Baptists in general are not known for speaking inconvenient and uncomfortable truth about racism, sexism (including homophobia), xenophobia, militarism, commercialism, and more.[14] Thus, Cooperative Baptists—along with others who follow the gospel of the extravagant generosity and radical hospitality shown in the ministry of Jesus—must now engage in tough thinking about prophetic choices and commitments on what it means to understand the demands of following Jesus. Stark differences exist between the ethics of Jesus and the ethics of President Trump—and should inspire followers of Jesus who believe in social justice to refuse to forsake Jesus in favor of the newly elected head of state.

For starters, followers of Jesus must decide whether to condemn white Christian nationalism as a heresy against the gospel of Jesus Christ. According to the New Testament, Jesus was a Palestinian Jew whose parents were immigrants in Egypt during his early life (Matthew 2:13-23). Jesus declared that refusal to welcome immigrants is refusal to welcome him (Matthew 25:43). If the prologue to the fourth Gospel is taken seriously, the Word—whom Cooperative Baptists and other evangelicals affirm—became incarnate in Jesus as "immigrant in chief" (John 1:1-18).

People who supported, voted for, and now cheer President Trump, while professing to be followers of the One who saves, must be challenged as committing heresy. White Christian nationalists, by supporting politicians and policies that oppress immigrants, demonstrate an irreconcilable contradiction. At best, their claims of allegiance to Jesus are ill-conceived. At worst, their claims of allegiance to Jesus are fraudulent. Any claim that one has welcomed the holy immigrant into one's heart and professed Jesus as the center of one's faith and living—while practicing xenophobia and other unwelcoming behaviors against other immigrants—is beyond unpersuasive. It is moral and ethical nonsense bordering on insanity.

White Christian nationalists who elected President Trump profess to follow Jesus. Yet Jesus affirmed and included women among his closest followers (Matthew 27:55-56), and they were the first to proclaim his resurrection (see Matthew 28:1-10). During the 2016 campaign, Trump bragged that his maleness, wealth, fame, and commercial success enabled and entitled him to sexually assault and disparage women.

Refusal to condemn white Christian nationalism as a heresy against the gospel of Jesus Christ amounts to affirming, even by inaction, allegiance to and support for President Trump and his threatening political policies and practices. Followers of Jesus cannot be faithful to the rule of President Trump and be faithful to the lordship of Jesus Christ. To be faithful to Jesus requires that we oppose Trump. As Dietrich Bonhoeffer wrote in the last century, the "costly grace" of the gospel of Jesus is first and always a call to discipleship to Jesus Christ, the Son of God.[15]

Jesus declared in the lesson of the Good Samaritan that the greatest commandment is to love God with one's entire being and to love others as oneself (Luke 10:25-37). This means that followers of Jesus must now, with the rest of the world watching, decide how to be prophetic followers of the Palestinian Jew whose parents migrated with him to Egypt to escape genocide. While the rest of the world watches, disciples of Christ must decide whether and how to operate twenty-first-century versions of the Underground Railroad and create a sanctuary movement in opposition to President Trump's campaign pledge to deport millions of undocumented immigrants. While the rest of the world watches, followers of Jesus must refuse to provide religious cover to Trump's policies towards people who are vulnerable.

The rest of the world will continue to watch to see if followers of Jesus are truly obedient to his call to lay down our lives to protect people who are poor, sick, racial minorities, Muslims, LGBTQ, disabled, laborers, and other targets of President Trump's oppressive campaign promises and executive policies (see Matthew 25:31-46).

Prophetic followers of Jesus must become more visible and vocal

The election of President Trump is clearly the latest, and perhaps the most ominous, test of our resolve as people of faith to fight what Dr. Cornel West has termed "the imperialist strain and plutocratic impulse in American life" in his book *Democracy Matters: Winning the Fight Against Imperialism.*[16] President Trump's rise to power reminds me of the following words by Dr. West:

> To be a Christian is to live dangerously, honestly, freely—to step in the name of love as if you may land on nothing, yet keep stepping because the something that sustains you no empire can give you and no empire can take away. This is the kind of vision and courage required to enable the renewal of prophetic, democratic Christian identity in the age of the American empire.[17]

As the Trump presidency unfolds, prophetic people must summon the courage to see clearly and speak honestly about justice, or more accurately, social injustice. Prophetic people from across the deep dimensions of humanity must throw off the shrouds of defeat, disappointment, dread, and dismay and turn to action, not mere reheated rhetoric. Learning from past mistakes, drawing courage from former victories, and reassembling forces and fortitude should be our goal. In this new but familiar season, the people who believe in redemptive love and social justice must embrace the mantles worn by Old Testament subversives, John the Baptist, Jesus, and those who followed Jesus in the tradition of the Old Testament subversives.

We must not repeat past errors of silence or offer muted protests when unjust practices and policies arise. Like the priest and Levite Jesus mentioned in the Good Samaritan lesson in Luke 10:29-37, many prophetic people "passed by on the other side of the road" after

Rodney King was brutally beaten by Los Angeles, California, police officers in 1991. Since then, too many Jesus-followers have been predictably mute despite recurring evidence that police brutality, racial profiling, and disparate policies are pervasive features of American law enforcement.

When the votes of poor and minority registrants were destroyed and not counted during the 2000 presidential election,[18] too many worshippers were conspicuously silent. Too many have said nothing as black, brown, poor and white, aged, student, and previously incarcerated persons have been routinely disenfranchised since the 2000 presidential election. For too many people, Bible studies on the biblical commandment against stealing failed to awaken prophetic consciousness, not to mention instill prophetic outrage about blatant, ongoing, and systemic efforts to deny marginalized people the right to vote.

We must also support those who struggle in the web and confines of the prison industrial complex and boldly condemn the systemic processes responsible for mass incarceration. Although churches, pastors, and lay people protest predatory payday lenders, similar attention has not been given to civil forfeiture practices and ancillary features of the ill-defined war against drugs, which allow the homes, money, and other property of people accused of committing drug offenses to be seized and declared forfeit before suspected drug offenders are convicted of any crime.[19]

As the nation's military adventures contribute to death and destruction in the long-running "war on terror," the national treasury is being drained of money that can stem the tide of income inequality, inadequate healthcare, homelessness, and other social needs. And religious global mission efforts, however well-intentioned, cannot soften the painful and ugly reality that too many of us have "passed by on the other side of the road."

We must no longer offer subdued and timid responses while voting rights are systematically and deliberately eroded and attacked. We must mount counter-measures to protect workers from mistreatment. These things are our solemn and committed duties as visible and vocal agents of God's justice. It is the obligation of God-loving people to stand in the gap to protect people from the bigotry sanctioned by legislative bodies. As congregations and faith-based organizations, our churches must lead by example and not be complicit in the blatant discrimination against unmarried people and those who are lesbian, gay, bisexual, and transgender. We, the people of God, must love God enough to hire and worship with followers of all orientations.

On these and other fronts, God's people must be instruments of courage and redemptive sacrifice for justice. We must stir ourselves out of a sense of crisis and show visionary courage to exemplify the power of God's liberating love. We must engage in the challenging, collective effort for justice to learn unpleasant truths, put aside longstanding myths, and develop relationships with those whom we have not previously taken the risk to know. Doing so will require willingness to embrace the realities and uncertainties associated with prophetic living and interactions.

I hope that, as people of faith, we affirm that Jesus and biblical and post-biblical prophets are compelling guides for a courageous and hopeful existence that requires willingness, as ministry partners, to endure the sacrifices of redemptive struggle against oppression and its intersecting realities. "If there is a cross for everyone," then each of us must understand that social injustice is an intersecting chain of oppression.

This means we must resist the temptation to ghettoize injustice. "Injustice anywhere is a threat to justice everywhere," said Ethiopia's Haile Selassie, followed years later by Dr. Martin Luther King Jr. The evil of the nation's commercial red-lining of black and brown neighborhoods is a variation of the same system that supported Israeli government actions to erect a wall separating West Bank Palestinians from Jerusalem. A threat that is constant cannot be met by an opposing force that is fearful, fitful, and fixated on localized oppression.

My prayer is that followers of Jesus will choose to meet the intersectionality of subjugation with the unconquerable force of love, as well as the determination to speak and move in prophetic truth. The 2016 election campaign and President Trump's success should be evidence that forces of repression are represented by people willing to take unjust actions. Those forces must be met and overcome by visible agents of God's peace, truth, and hope.

Prophetic activism requires throwing off moral and ethical dwarfism

Donald Trump's election surprised the professional pundits who game US politics. But Trump is not a novelty. Proponents of political pietism and Christian quietism have courted favor with, enabled, and supported racist, sexist, imperialistic, xenophobic, homophobic, and brutal politicians at every period of US history.

The United States Constitution is perhaps the best evidence of this point. Article I, Section 2 of the document that took effect in 1787 gave slave-holding states preferential treatment in the House of Representatives. According to Article I, Section 7, all legislation for raising revenue must originate in the House of Representatives. Article I, Section 9 contains the following chilling provision: "The Migration of Importation of such Persons as any of the States now existing shall think proper to admit, shall not be prohibited by the Congress prior to the Year one thousand eight hundred and eight [1808], but a tax or duty may be imposed on such Importation, not exceeding ten dollars [$10.00] for each Person." The Founders placed racism, white supremacy, imperialism, human trafficking, and capitalist idolatry in the political and ethical DNA of the United States from the beginning of our nation. Prophetic followers of Jesus should mention that when politicians and pundits brag about "American exceptionalism." Political pietism and Christian quietism watched it, was complicit in it, and sacralized it.

Prophetic integrity compels one to admit that political pietists and Christian quietists turned a blind eye to state-sanctioned injustice as Africans were subjected to human trafficking, kidnapping, rape, torture, and murder in support of slavery. Political pietists and Christian quietists stood by, like the priest and Levite in the Good Samaritan lesson found in Luke's Gospel (see Luke 10:25-37), when Native Americans were brutalized, harassed, robbed, and forcibly removed from ancestral lands their people had occupied for generations before President Andrew Jackson's administration force-marched them along what is now called the Trail of Tears between southeastern states and Oklahoma.[20]

Political pietists and Christian quietists stood by as political predecessors to Donald Trump and Senator Jeff Sessions waged war against Mexico and sanctioned outright land theft from Spanish-speaking people who lived west of the Mississippi River.[21] Political pietism and Christian quietism gave tacit consent or active support to those predecessors to Donald Trump who practiced human trafficking, wage theft, land theft, and other acts of xenophobic bigotry against Chinese immigrants.[22] Political pietism and Christian quietism consented to and enabled racist policies and practices against Japanese immigrants.[23]

Followers of Jesus must, therefore, challenge this society with the truth of Allan Boesak's observation that "Donald Trump is not a new, alien phenomenon that has fallen out of the clear blue sky. He is . . . the logical and inevitable consequence of American politics. . . ."[24] Now followers of Jesus must decide whether to mimic the behavior of past political pietists and Christian quietists across the landscape of US history, or to obey the call to Ezekiel to speak truth to President Donald Trump, the latest leader of the "rebellious house" that heralds itself with self-righteous arrogance as "the land of the free and the home of the brave."

Discussion and Reflection Questions

1. When has your Bible study group, Sunday school class, or congregation acted as agents and instruments of the radical, inclusive, and generous love of God in the face of social justice ills in your community? What was the result?

2. How have "good" evangelical Christians shown or stated that their political stances are different from persons who are considered more inclusive?

3. When have you challenged "good" white evangelical Christians whose voting behavior resembles positions and actions taken by white Christian nationalists?

4. How have you and the followers of Jesus with whom you most closely or often identify become "more visible and vocal" about social injustice in your community?

Notes

1. The material in this chapter largely expands on an essay I wrote for a special issue of the Cooperative Baptist Fellowship of Arkansas newsletter at the invitation of CBFAR Moderator Dr. Patricia Griffen (my wife) and CBFAR Coordinator Dr. Ray Higgins. I thank them for encouraging me to take what was too lengthy for a newsletter and offer it to a wider audience.

2. See www.bbc.com/news/election-us-2016-37922587, accessed January 9, 2017.

3. See www.bbc.com/news/election-us-2016-37922587, accessed January 9, 2017.

4. See religiondispatches.org/douthat-the-good-christians-reject-trump/. Also see www.newyorker.com/magazine/2015/08/31/the-fearful-and-the-frustrated. Both accessed January 9, 2017.

5. Daniel Hummel has traced how, religiously and politically, revivalist nationalism evolved into what is now evangelical nationalism in an article titled "Revivalist Nationalism Since WWII: From 'Wake Up, America!' to 'Make America Great Again.'" See www.mdpi.com/2077-1444/7/11/128//, accessed January 9, 2017.

6. See www.thenation.com/article/eighty-one-percent-of-white-evangelicals-voted-for-donald-trump-why/, accessed January 9, 2017.

7. The Public Religion Research Institute (PRRI) report of September 22, 2016 can be viewed at www.prri.org/wp-content/uploads/2016/09/PRRI-RNS-Unaffiliated-Report.pdf, accessed January 9, 2017.

8. Allan Aubrey Boesak and Curtiss Paul DeYoung, *Radical Reconciliation: Beyond Political Pietism and Christian Quietism* (Maryknoll, NY: Orbis Books, 2012), 1.

9. See November 4, 2016, *New York Times* front page article titled "In Poll, Voters Express Disgust in U.S. Politics" at www.nytimes.com/2016/11/04/us/politics/hillary-clinton-donald-trump-poll.html, accessed January 9, 2017.

10. See www.nytimes.com/2016/11/15/opinion/turn-on-the-hate-steve-bannon-at-the-white-house.html, accessed January 9, 2017.

11. See www.theguardian.com/commentisfree/cifamerica/2009/may/05/jeff-sessions-arlen-specter-judiciary-committee, accessed January 9, 2017.

12. See www.nytimes.com/2016/11/13/nyregion/giulianis-gamble-on-trump-pays-off-bigly.html, accessed January 9, 2017.

13. See www.washingtonpost.com/news/the-fix/wp/2016/09/21/it-looks-like-rudy-giuliani-convinced-donald-trump-that-stop-and-frisk-actually-works/, accessed January 9, 2017.

14. This observation does not disregard the prophetic examples of people such as Foy Valentine, T.B. Maston, Robert U. Ferguson, President Jimmy and First Lady Rosalyn Carter, James Dunn, and others. However, those examples are exceptions to the record of Cooperative Baptist witness concerning social justice.

15. See Dietrich Bonhoeffer, *The Cost of Discipleship*, rev. ed. (New York: Macmillan Publishing Co., 1963).

16. Cornel West, *Democracy Matters: Winning the Fight Against Imperialism* (New York: Penguin Press, 2004), 3.

17. See West, supra, 172 (emphasis added). Dr. West defined Constantinian Christianity, distinguished it from prophetic Christianity, and described the progression of Constantinian Christianity and American notions of empire in Chapter 5 of *Democracy Matters*.

18. See www.sfgate.com/opinion/article/1-million-black-votes-didn-t-count-in-the-2000-2747895.php, accessed January 9, 2017.

19. See www.theatlantic.com/politics/archive/2015/05/the-glaring-injustice-of-civil-asset-forfeiture/392999/, accessed January 9, 2017.

20. See www.history.com/topics/native-american-history/trail-of-tears, accessed January 9, 2017.

21. See www.houstonculture.org/hispanic/conquest4.html, accessed January 9, 2017.

22. See www.zakkeith.com/articles,blogs,forums/anti-Chinese-persecution-in-the-USA-history-timeline.htm, accessed January 9, 2017.

23. See immigrationtounitedstates.org/348-anti-japanese-movement.html, accessed January 9, 2017.

24. Allan Boesak shared this observation in a November 15, 2016, email exchange with me.

CHAPTER 3

What's Love Got to Do with It?
Confronting Our Issues of Prophetic Discipleship[1]

Beware of false prophets, who come to you in sheep's clothing but inwardly are ravenous wolves. You will know them by their fruits. —Matthew 7:15-16

The election of Donald Trump is the latest and most compelling reason that followers of Jesus have for facing the theological, hermeneutical, and ethical deficiencies that contribute to our inability or refusal to better understand the clear mandate of Jesus. Our long-cherished religious liberty must coexist alongside and be integral to a commitment to equality and social justice because of the gospel of Jesus (see Luke 10:25-37).

My fundamental premise is that evangelical followers of Jesus have not considered social justice to be part of the deep and wide salvation theme that runs throughout Scripture. This shortcoming is because the Hebrew and New Testaments are not studied, preached, or understood as valuable social justice source material. In much the same way, evangelicals have refused to understand that those sacred writings declare salvation to be a social justice imperative.

Consequently, most evangelical followers of Jesus affirm faith without a biblical appreciation of the relationship between discipleship and social justice. Failure to include social justice as fundamental to and inseparable from salvation and discipleship hinders the ability of evangelical followers of Jesus to develop and live out a robust social ethic consistent with the teachings of Jesus and the social justice imperative found in the Hebrew and New Testaments.

The Traditional Evangelical Approach to Social Justice—Religious Freedom

The freedom of a person or community to publicly or privately manifest religious beliefs or teach, practice, worship, and otherwise observe religious traditions—including the freedom not to follow any religion—has long been considered a fundamental human right in various societies across the ages. In a country with a state religion, religious liberty contemplates that the government permits other sects aside from the state religion and does not persecute believers of other faiths.

Many, if not most, evangelical followers of Jesus view religious liberty in the United States from the perspectives of Western European and US history. Protestants will trace their views on religious liberty to 1517, when Martin Luther published his famous Ninety-five Theses in Wittenberg in an effort to reform Catholicism. Luther was given an opportunity to recant at the Diet of Worms before Charles V, the holy Roman emperor. Luther refused to recant, was declared a heretic, and was then sequestered in the Wartburg Castle, where he translated the New Testament into German. After Luther was excommunicated by Papal Bull in 1521, the Reformation movement gained ground, spread to Switzerland, and then grew to England, France, and elsewhere in Europe.

The French Revolution abolished state religion in France. However, all property of the Roman Catholic Church was confiscated, and intolerance against Catholics ensued. Under Calvinist leadership, the Netherlands became the most religiously tolerant country in Europe by granting asylum to persecuted religious minorities (French Huguenots, English Dissenters, and Jews expelled from Spain and Portugal).[2]

Religious freedom began in the Netherlands and New Amsterdam (now New York) during the Dutch Republic. When New Amsterdam surrendered to the English in 1664, freedom of religion was guaranteed in the Articles of Capitulation. That freedom also benefited Jews who arrived on Manhattan Island in 1654 after fleeing Portuguese persecution in Brazil. Other Jewish communities were eventually established during the eighteenth century in Philadelphia, Charleston, Savannah, Richmond (Virginia), and Newport (Rhode Island).[3]

Efforts to escape religious intolerance are part of our national heritage. Recall that the Pilgrims first sought refuge from religious persecution in the Netherlands and later founded Plymouth Colony in Massachusetts in 1620. However, most of the early colonies were not generally tolerant of religious pluralism, with the notable exception of Maryland. The colony of Maryland, founded by Lord Baltimore, a Catholic, was the first government in what eventually became the United States to formally recognize freedom of religion in 1634.[4]

Roger Williams was forced to establish the new colony of Rhode Island to escape religious persecution driven by the Puritan theocracy in Massachusetts. Massachusetts Bay Colony Puritans were active persecutors of Quakers, along with Puritans in Plymouth Colony and other colonies along the Connecticut River.[5]

In 1660 an English Quaker named Mary Dyer was hanged in Boston, Massachusetts, for repeatedly defying a Puritan law that banned Quakers from the colony. Her hanging marked the beginning of the end of the Puritan theocracy and New England independence from English rule, as King Charles II in 1661 prohibited Massachusetts from executing anyone for professing Quakerism.[6]

Students of US history, and particularly religious liberty, are no doubt familiar with William Penn. Chief Justice Earl Warren summed up Penn's courageous commitment to religious liberty in his book *A Republic, If You Can Keep It*. William Penn was a Quaker leader in London. The Quakers were not recognized by the government and were forbidden to meet in any building for worship. In 1681 King Charles II of England gave the Pennsylvania region (Pennsylvania means "Penn's Woods") to William Penn, a Quaker, who established the Pennsylvania colony so that Quakers and other faiths could have religious freedom.[7]

These and other historical events, along with the First and Fourteenth Amendments to the US Constitution, form the foundation for what many people, including followers of Jesus, understand about religious liberty. The First Amendment, ratified in 1791, reads, in pertinent part, that "Congress shall make no law respecting an establishment of religion, or prohibiting the free exercise thereof . . . ."[8]

That constitutional guarantee was later made applicable to the United States through the Fourteenth Amendment.[9] The Fourteenth Amendment states that "no State shall make or enforce any law which shall abridge the privileges or immunities of citizens of the United States; nor shall any State deprive any person of life, liberty, or property, without due process of law; nor deny to any person within its jurisdiction the equal protection of the laws."[10] Together, the First and Fourteenth Amendments guarantee that government will not establish a religion, prefer one religion over another, become entangled in disputes involving religious doctrine, practices, and officials, or interfere with the "free exercise" of religion.

However, the religious liberty ideal has biblical antecedents in the Hebrew Testament, the Gospels of Jesus, and the rest of the New Testament.

Religious Liberty Antecedents in the Hebrew Testament

We read in Genesis 41 that Joseph, a great grandson of Abraham, became prominent in Egypt when his spiritual discernment was recognized because he interpreted an Egyptian pharaoh's dreams as an omen of approaching years of agricultural prosperity followed by years of famine (Genesis 41:1-45). The dramatic narrative in Genesis 43:26-34 about Joseph recognizing his brother Benjamin becomes even more meaningful when we read that the Egyptians who dined with Joseph "ate with him by themselves"—apart from Joseph (their esteemed prime minister) and apart from Joseph's brothers—"because the Egyptians could not eat with the Hebrews, for that is an abomination to the Egyptians" (Genesis 43:32). Joseph rose to political prominence in Egyptian society due to his spiritual discernment of the king's dream. Nevertheless, the social separation described in that dining narrative indicates that Joseph had something resembling a "separate but equal" coexistence with his fellow Egyptian political operatives. Joseph is recognized in the final chapters of Genesis as a man whose religious values and ethnic identity set him apart in Egyptian society.

Exodus, the second book in the Hebrew canon, opens with the dramatic story of how the Hebrew people were socially, economically, and politically oppressed by the Egyptian majority. We traditionally have understood the Exodus as the salvation narrative of the Hebrew people from Egyptian bondage. However, the Exodus narrative also exposes a struggle for religious, social, and physical liberty in the collision between the religious, political, social, and ethical framework of the Egyptian empire and the liberating design of God presented through the agency of Moses and his brother, Aaron. As the editors of the *New Oxford Annotated Bible* note:

> The predictability, the timing of both beginning and ending, the intensity, the contest between Aaron and the [Egyptian] magicians, the distinction between Egyptians and Israelites, and the emphasis on Pharaoh's knowing (acknowledging) God all point to combat on two interrelated levels: between Israel's God and Egypt's gods (12.12), including the deified Pharaoh, and between their human representatives, Moses and Aaron, and Pharaoh, his officials, and his magicians.[11]

Exodus is also a vivid illustration about the quest for religious liberty and the collision of divergent systems of religious belief. Moses was sent to Egypt to present a divine demand to the Pharaoh that the Israelites be freed so that they could worship their God (see Exodus 10:3-4). During the series of plagues Pharaoh's courtiers appealed on one occasion for their leader to allow the Israelites to go, saying: "How long shall this fellow [Moses] be a snare to us? Let the people go, so that they may worship the LORD their God" (Exodus 10:7).

Deuteronomy should also be understood for its relevance to our understanding of religious liberty and justice. The Israelites entered Canaan bent on genocide of the indigenous population based on the view that nothing short of that would allow them to be a holy people (see Deuteronomy 7:1-7,16-26).

From Judges onward, the Hebrew canon presents numerous accounts of political, military, and social collisions between followers of the religion of Moses and neighboring societies known for different religious beliefs and practices. And the writings concerning the Hebrew prophets from Elijah forward contain vivid accounts of competing, and often violent, religious claims, ranging from the standoff between Elijah and the priests of Baal on Mount Carmel (see 1 Kings 18:17-46) to the threats and dangers suffered by Jeremiah from other politically favored religious figures of his time (see Jeremiah 38:1-13).

Religious liberty is a theme dramatically presented in the post-exilic writings of the Hebrew canon. Like Joseph in Egypt, Daniel, Hananiah, Mishael, and Azariah preserved their ethnic and religious identity after they were taken to Babylon (see Daniel 1:3-20). The fiery furnace experience of Hananiah (Shadrach), Mishael (Meshach), and Azariah (Abednego) we read about in Daniel 3 and the lion's den experience of Daniel in Daniel 6 are plainly lessons about civil disobedience based on religious devotion.

Some commentators view the historical novella of Esther, and particularly the title character, as representative of "the marginal and sometimes precarious status of Diaspora Jews who were obliged to accommodate their lives to an alien environment" in a way that "differs markedly from the outlook of Diaspora Jews like Ezra and Nehemiah."[12] That is not only an observation about religious liberty. The Book of Esther is fundamentally about social justice concerns involving patriarchy, male supremacy, the objectification of women as objects of male sexual pleasure, and treatment of immigrants. Unfortunately, those issues are rarely mentioned by commentators, preachers, and religious educators.

Religious Liberty Antecedents in the Gospels

The Gospels of Jesus present numerous illustrations of divergent religious systems engaged in a more or less uneasy coexistence that exposed dramatic societal inequities. The Jewish people of Palestine lived under Roman political and military control yet retained the freedom to follow their religious traditions.

However, the Gospels also demonstrate the challenges that ensue when a minority religious movement (the religion of Jesus) attempts to coexist alongside a dominant religious tradition (that of the Sanhedrin Council orthodoxy). The contrast between how Jesus understood and applied the moral, social, and ethical imperatives of Torah and how Torah was understood and applied by established and recognized religious leaders of his time and place runs throughout the Gospels.

The sharp difference between the religion of Jesus and the religious perspective of the scribes and Pharisees resulted in clashes between Jesus, followers of Jesus, and unnamed critics. In Mark 9 we read that Jesus found his disciples and "some scribes" arguing in the same passage where Jesus healed a boy afflicted by what the text terms "an unclean spirit" (see Mark 9:14-19). That passage involved the social justice issue of healthcare for a sick child *and* the religious liberty concern posed by the religion of Jesus in the face of the established religious regime.

Religious liberty *and* social justice—not religious liberty alone—is a recurring theme in the Gospels. We read in Luke's Gospel that when disciples of Jesus tried to stop an anonymous exorcist from casting out demons, Jesus contradicted their intolerance, saying, "Do not stop him; for whoever is not against you is for you" (see Mark 9:14-19). The nighttime meeting between Jesus and Nicodemus vividly demonstrates an attempt at intrafaith dialogue (see John 3:1-21). The encounter between Jesus and the woman of Samaria at Jacob's Well is a similar encounter. The social justice impetus of Jesus included an aspect of religious liberty that impelled him to push aside longstanding sectarian and ethnic animosities, as well as patriarchy and male supremacy, in pursuit of redemptive fellowship (see John 4:1-42).

The Johannine community, to which we owe the Gospel of John, appears to have understood the religion of Jesus as a minority movement that threatened the religious, political, cultural, and social hegemony of the Sanhedrin Council, especially after the raising of Lazarus (see John 11:45–12:11). When we read about the trial of Jesus before the Sanhedrin Council and his subsequent indictment by the Sanhedrin before Pontius Pilate, the Roman governor, we are not only reading how religious figures in a dominant religion fabricated a national security accusation to stamp out the emerging religion of Jesus. We are also reading about how a dominant religious faction collaborated with the political regime to brand Jesus an enemy of the state in much the same way that white Christian nationalists and Donald Trump joined forces to brand Muslims as national security threats in their quest to lay hold of the US presidency.

According to John's Gospel, Pilate was not interested in refereeing a religious dispute between rival Palestinian Jewish factions, so he tried to release Jesus. However, when Sanhedrin leaders falsely accused Jesus with insurrection, Pilate lost interest in achieving liberty for Jesus and ordered him crucified (see John 18:28–19:16). We rarely, if ever, hear the crucifixion of Jesus interpreted for its political and social justice significance alongside the traditional salvation perspective.

Religious Liberty Challenges from Acts to Revelation

We do not proceed far in the book of Acts before the religion of Jesus collides again with the dominant religious movement in Jerusalem. Peter and John were arrested and brought before the Sanhedrin Council after they healed a lame man and proclaimed that the man was healed "by the name of Jesus Christ of Nazareth, whom you crucified . . ." (Acts 4:10). Again, notice how religious liberty becomes relevant because followers of Jesus engaged in healthcare, a social justice concern. As the religion of Jesus began attracting more followers, the threats that Peter and John received turned into sectarian persecution, as shown by the trial and stoning of Stephen (see Acts 6:7–8:1).

We read about the encounter between Philip and the Ethiopian eunuch in Acts 8 and are accustomed to that passage being highlighted for its evangelism and missionary significance. Yet the passage is equally instructive concerning social justice.

Philip fled Jerusalem after the stoning of Stephen and went to the city of Samaria. His presence and ministry effort there were not merely tolerated but were so well received that Peter and John, dispatched from Jerusalem to investigate, were also welcomed. These are clear examples of immigration and inclusion events in the lives of early followers of Jesus (see Acts 8:4-25).

We do not gain a complete perspective about the conversion of Saul of Tarsus if we disregard that Saul was a leading force in the effort to root out and exterminate followers of Jesus. Saul's opposition to religious liberty deserves to be highlighted. We should also emphasize that his effort to stamp out the religion of Jesus resulted in social injustice.

After Saul was converted, he was accepted by the Damascus community of Jesus followers (see Acts 1–22). When we read in Acts 9 that "the church throughout Judea, Galilee, and Samaria had peace," "was built up," and "increased in numbers" (Acts 9:31), we may reasonably argue that the religion of Jesus traces its early ascendance to conflicts, challenges, and victories surrounding the exercise of religious liberty and the challenge of doing justice.

Beginning in Acts 10, we read how early followers of Jesus began to struggle among themselves with divergent viewpoints. Peter's rooftop vision and later baptism of Cornelius (see Acts 10) eventually forced the young religious movement to become ethnically inclusive.

By the time we reach Acts 15, that inclusivity was being challenged by traditionalists who insisted that Gentile followers of Jesus become circumcised. The council we read about at Antioch in Acts 15 shows how the young movement wrestled with divergent religious views among its own adherents and struggled to coexist alongside the religious teachings and practices of the Sanhedrin Council, all while living as colonized people under Roman political and military occupation. These are plainly social justice concerns.

When we read in Acts 16 about Paul and Silas then being jailed in Philippi, we are reading about a religious liberty struggle involving unjust incarceration (see Acts 16:11-40). When we read that Paul and Silas were accused of "turning the world upside down" during their brief ministry in Thessalonica (see Acts 17:1-9, especially v. 6), and when we read elsewhere in Acts and other New Testament epistles about the imprisonment, trials, and other experiences of Paul during his missionary efforts, we are reading how the religion of Jesus was threatened and oppressed by the dominant religious faction. The New Testament closes with the Revelation of John, who wrote that he was exiled on the island of Patmos in the Aegean Sea "because of the word of God and the testimony of Jesus" (see Revelation 1:9).

The Cost of Ignoring Biblical Religious Liberty Antecedents

Evangelical followers of Jesus are not nurtured to recognize these and other religious liberty and social justice illustrations in our sacred writings. This demonstrates a glaring shortcoming in the traditional ways evangelicals engage theology, hermeneutics, and ethics.

I agree with proponents of liberation theology who argue that the Bible presents God as suffering alongside oppressed people. When God confronted Moses for the first time in Exodus, God identified with enslaved people, not the empire that oppressed them, as shown by the following memorable passage:

> Then the LORD said, "I have observed the misery of my people who are in Egypt; I have heard their cry on account of their taskmasters. Indeed, I know their sufferings, and I have come down to deliver them from the Egyptians, and to bring them up out of that land to a good and broad land, a land flowing with milk and honey, to the country of the Canaanites, the Hittites, the Amorites, the Perizzites, the Hivites, and the Jebusites. The cry of the Israelites has now come to me; I have also seen how the Egyptians oppress them. So come, I will send you to Pharaoh to bring my people, the Israelites, out of Egypt." (Exodus 3:7-10)

Professor Theodore Walker Jr. has observed that black liberation theology "understands that liberating answers to questions pertaining to the circumstance of oppression and the struggle for freedom are essential to the Christian witness," resulting in "a particular vision of God that has been summarily formulated by James Cone and others under the conception of God as 'God of the oppressed.' " Walker explains that vision of God and contrasts it against what he termed "the prevailing Western theological tradition" as follows:

> To be sure, black theology is defined in considerable measure by its protest against the prevailing Western theological tradition. History has taught us that classical Western theism is quite capable of abiding peaceably with, and even of being very supportive of, such oppressive activities as the enslavement of Africans and the genocide of Native Americans. It is characteristic of black theology to be unforgivingly critical of any theology that fails to affirm that God favors the struggle for liberation. If God is conceived so as not to favor this struggle, then God is thereby conceived so as not to experience fully our pain and suffering. Such a conception of God is contrary to the Christian witness to God's suffering as indicated by the cross, and it is contrary to the vision of God as that utterly unsurpassable *Friend* whose love is perfect and all-inclusive. . . .[13]

One's perspective on theology (the nature and meaning of God) affects hermeneutics (how people interpret Scripture). The evangelical hermeneutic is based on what Walker terms "the prevailing classical Western [white] theism," which has traditionally resulted in emphasis on piety and personal salvation, global evangelism, and missions. Evangelicals frequently cite the Great Commission passage (Matthew 28:19-20) as authority for that emphasis. Sadly, the theological and hermeneutical perspectives of evangelicals have also been allied with maintaining oppressive order, not achieving liberation from oppression.

This tendency is, to some extent, responsible for cognitive dissonance—morally and ethically—among evangelicals concerning religious liberty and other biblical imperatives regarding justice. Because they have not interpreted the Bible in terms of its relevance to social justice in general and liberty, including (but by no means limited to) religious liberty, evangelicals primarily consider religious liberty an essential attribute for a well-ordered society, not a moral and ethical imperative arising from the divine passion for liberation from all forms of oppression.

Martin Luther King Jr. reflected on the ethical and social consequences of Western theism to some extent in his famous "Letter from a Birmingham Jail." Ponder this excerpt from King's letter of April 16, 1963 to white Birmingham clerics who criticized him for becoming involved in nonviolent civil disobedience efforts to protest racial segregation in Birmingham, Alabama:

> So often the contemporary church is a weak, ineffectual voice with an uncertain sound. So often it is an arch-defender of the status quo. Far from being disturbed by the presence of the church, the power structure of the average community is consoled by the church's silent—and often even vocal—sanction of things as they are.[14]

More than half a century has passed since King's letter. However, his observations are, sadly, still true today. Last year, I and others received an email message from Rev. Daniel Buford, Minister of Justice at Allen Temple Baptist Church in Oakland, California, that echoed King's assessment. In pertinent part, it reads as follows:

> This morning I had an "Aha!" moment of epiphany. . . . Black people are the canaries in the mineshafts of institutional racism; what kills us mostly and firstly will kill everyone eventually regardless of race. Our problem is compounded by the fact that we are also trapped in a labyrinth with the Minotaur of white supremacist state sponsored terrorism. . . . People . . . don't give a damn about stopping rogue police as long as Blacks and Mexicans are mainly being hunted. . . ."[15]

Although theologians and evangelical leaders profess belief in religious liberty, they somehow have consistently lacked the theological and ethical capacity to relate religious liberty to the wider struggle for freedom from oppression. As Rev. Buford shared in his email message, this demonstrates a basic deficiency in human empathy. I call it moral and ethical dwarfism. The fact that 81 percent of evangelical Christians voted for Donald Trump proves that moral and ethical dwarfism is pervasive among white Christian nationalists.

I see no evidence that more than a few evangelicals recognize, respect, support, and have joined the Black Lives Matter movement and struggle for freedom from the oppression of state-sanctioned abuse and homicide of black people by law enforcement officials. Likewise, immigrants facing xenophobic rhetoric from talk-show commentators and self-serving politicians see little evidence, if any, that evangelical scholars, congregational leaders, and rank-and-file evangelicals consider their plight in the face of blatant oppression to be relevant. Workers struggling for living wages see little evidence that evangelicals who are adamant about religious liberty consider income inequality to be morally and ethically relevant to the evangelical notion of justice.

The defect in human empathy arising from theological, hermeneutical, and ethical parochialism explains how evangelicals can be alarmed that photographers, bakers, florists, and a Kentucky county clerk must serve all persons, while US evangelical pastors support oppression of LGBTQ persons in Uganda.[16] Moral and ethical dwarfism accounts for the incongruity between evangelical complaints about religious persecution of Christians in China,[17] contrasted by their appalling silence, if not open endorsement, of Israeli-government-sanctioned persecution of and discrimination against Arabs and followers of Jesus in Israel.[18]

I attribute moral and ethical dwarfism of evangelicals regarding religious liberty and social justice to the theological, hermeneutical, and ethical failure of evangelical scholars, denominational leaders, and pastors. They study, preach, and teach the Hebrew Testament account of Naomi returning to Judah from Moab after the deaths of her husband and sons (see Ruth 1). Yet, somehow, they are unable or unwilling to recognize and affirm the theological, hermeneutical, and ethical relevance of that passage to demands by Palestinians to return to land from which they have been displaced.

Evangelical scholars, denominational leaders, and pastors study, preach, and teach the Hebrew Testament account of how Queen Jezebel of Samaria orchestrated a state-sponsored land grab of the vineyard of Naboth, the Jezreelite (see 1 Kings 21:1-19). Somehow, that scholarship, preaching, and teaching fails to illuminate and affirm the theological, moral, and ethical relevance of this biblical passage to Israeli-government displacement of Palestinians from their homes, destruction of Palestinian crops and farm land, and construction of illegal Jewish settlements.[19]

These and numerous other examples are why people struggling against oppressive power view the claims of evangelicals about religious liberty with disappointment, mounting distrust, and even disgust. People struggling against oppression have good reason for that disappointment, distrust, and disgust. They understand that their struggle for liberation from oppression is grounded in belief that God is, to quote again the words of Theodore Walker Jr., "that utterly unsurpassable *Friend* whose love is perfect and all-inclusive."

Although evangelicals are viewed as the dominant sect among followers of Jesus, evangelicals appear not only intolerant toward other religions; they also appear insensitive, if not unsympathetic and disdainful, about oppression faced by others. There is scant evidence from the course offerings I read on the websites of evangelical seminaries that many of the evangelical scholars who teach and write about religious liberty care about people suffering from mass incarceration, terrorism due to racial profiling, race-based abusive and homicidal police conduct, xenophobia, homophobia, economic oppression caused by classism and capitalism, and other kinds of oppression. Instead, it seems that evangelical scholars, pastors, and other leaders care about religious liberty only because they want to be free to proselytize their version of the religion of Jesus, not because they believe God cares about liberating all people who suffer from any oppression.

This shortcoming matters more than one might think. Recall that the early followers of Jesus were a minority sect. When Constantine became the first Roman emperor to claim conversion to Christianity, the religion of Jesus entered the mainstream. The Inquisition and Protestant Reformation show that, even as followers of Jesus struggled across time to demonstrate tolerance for divergent views within our own belief system, they committed, condoned, or ignored blatant atrocities against people and claimed the moral right to do so from God.

However, the Bible shows that God is not concerned only that people are free to proselytize. Our sacred writings also illuminate God's concern that people be free to live, work, and be accepted where they live as persons of dignity and worth, not considered deviants, threats, or commodities for private and social exploitation.

In 2015 President Marvin McMickle of Colgate-Rochester Divinity School concluded a stirring address with the following statement:

> I believe in the First Amendment, in the separation of church and state, in religious liberty, and in the right to worship God as one chooses or not to worship God at all. However, I believe in something else just as strongly; maybe more so. . . . I believe that our nation has not yet resolved all of the lingering effects of nearly 400 years of slavery, segregation, and second-class status for millions of its citizens. All of this was done and continues to be done by the activity of many who represent the power of the state. Sadly, it could not have lasted as long as it has if it had not been for the silence of so many of those who represent the message of the church, the synagogue, and the mosque.
>
> Borrowing a line from the 1960s song by Simon and Garfunkel, I hope the day will come when the church in America will break the "Sound of Silence" in the face of injustice and inequality! I believe in religious liberty, and I hope that all who labor for the separation of church and state as a valid principle in American society will also labor for the civil and human rights

of those whose quest for physical freedom has lasted just as long as the fight for freedom of conscience.[20]

I join Dr. McMickle in urging evangelical followers of Jesus to break from the morally and ethically indefensible dwarfish practice of supporting "soul liberty" while actively opposing the demands from others for life, liberty, and equality. The love of God about which we preach, study, sing, write, teach, and pray demands that followers of Jesus love God enough to protect our neighbors, including our neighbors with divergent lives, beliefs, behaviors, and struggles, as much as we cherish our own religious liberty.

Most evangelical seminaries, denominational leaders, other religious educators, and pastors have refused to embrace a vision of God that affirms robust respect for and advocacy of social justice, along with religious freedom, to be a fundamental and inseparable part of a deeper and wider reverence for God's involvement in and support for the human struggle for liberation. That shortcoming blinds evangelicals morally; it also hinders evangelicals ethically from recognizing and affirming that others must be protected from *any* persecution, mistreatment, bigotry, and other oppression, not merely religious-based persecution, mistreatment, bigotry, and oppression.

Consequently, we should not be surprised when evangelical followers of Jesus misunderstand, and misrepresent, the social justice imperative enshrined in the First and Fourteenth Amendments, the equality guarantee of the Fourteenth Amendment, and the "love of neighbor" ethic taught and lived by Jesus. And, as Martin Luther King Jr. pointedly observed to religious leaders considered "moderates" more than fifty years ago from a Birmingham jail, we should not be surprised by people "whose disappointment with the church has risen to outright disgust."

The people who teach theology, hermeneutics, and ethics must call followers of Jesus to participate with God in the divine struggle for human dignity and equality concerning matters beyond the freedom to proselytize, pray, preach, and erect monuments to those efforts. Religious liberty is a fundamental social justice imperative based on a deeper and wider understanding about who God is and what God is about, not merely a tool used to achieve national pluralism based on tolerance of divergent sectarian beliefs and practices.

Hence, evangelicals must rethink theology, hermeneutics, and ethics. If evangelical followers of Jesus are to develop and live a mature and robust faith—a faith not defined by moral and ethical dwarfism—then the people who teach theology, hermeneutics, and ethics, the people who lead religious denominations, and the people who lead congregations must hold, and affirm, a vision that God participates in the human struggle for liberation from oppression in all its forms.

Respect for religious liberty must be understood, affirmed, and based on the deeper and wider love of God, the love that inspires one to recognize and respect the inherent dignity and equality of all persons. Until evangelicals ground our notions of religious liberty in the deeper and wider love of God, our religious liberty advocacy and rhetoric will be correctly recognized, and ultimately dismissed, as sectarian chauvinism.

According to what Jesus said in (Matthew 7:15-17, God deserves much better than that from us. And the author of 1 John 4 understood what it means when people who claim to love God deliberately oppress others:

> Beloved, let us love one another, because love is from God; everyone who loves is born of God and knows God. Whoever does not love does not know God, for God is love. . . . No one has ever seen God; if we love one another, God lives in us, and his love is perfected in us. . . . Love has been perfected among us in this: that we may have boldness on the day of judgment, because as he is, so are we in this world. There is no fear in love, but perfect love casts out fear; for fear has to do with punishment, and whoever fears has not reached perfection in love. We love because he first loved us. Those who say, "I love God," and hate their brothers or sisters, are liars; for those who do not love a brother or sister whom they have seen, cannot love God whom they have not seen. The commandment we have from him is

this: those who love God must love their brothers and sisters also. (1 John 4:7-8,12,7-21)

Discussion and Reflection Questions

1. To what extent was concern about social justice and the exercise of power in relationships a factor in how you became a follower of Jesus? When and how did you recognize that social justice and the way power is obtained in relationships are factors in the meaning of "salvation"?

2. How do those in your faith settings address matters such as racial injustice, male privilege, militarism, materialism, and environmental justice? How do they address animosity toward and mistreatment of immigrants? Are they concerned about persons who are imprisoned or persons who are vulnerable due to disease, injury, infirmity, or age (young or old)?

3. In what ways can your faith community and other followers of Jesus resist and overcome the presence and effects of moral and ethical dwarfism?

Notes

1. I presented the ideas in this chapter at Fuller Theological Seminary in California during the inaugural Baptist Joint Committee Lectures on Religious Liberty in November 2015. I am grateful to Brent Walker and Charles Watson of the Baptist Joint Committee for the opportunity. Given that 81 percent of evangelical Christians voted for Donald Trump, my observations take on new relevance.

2. Karl Heussi, *Kompendium der Kirchengeschichte*, 11. Auflage (1956), Tubingen (Germany), 396–397.

3. Clifton E. Olmstead, *History of Religion in the United States* (Englewood Cliffs, NJ: Prentice-Hall, 1960), 124.

4. Mark Zimmerman, "Symbol of Enduring Freedom," *Columbia* Magazine, March 2010, 19. Although freedom of religion was first established as a principle of government in the colony of Maryland in 1634, it was not continuously respected from that time forward. Full religious liberty would not remain in Maryland until 1776, when Charles Carroll of Maryland signed the Declaration of Independence. See Kenneth L. Lasson (2016) "Religious Freedom and the Church-State Relationship in Maryland," *The Catholic Lawyer*: Vol. 14: No. 1, Article 3. Available at: http://scholarship.law.stjohns.edu/tcl/vol14/iss1/3.

5. See Horatio Rogers, *Mary Dyer of Rhode Island: The Quaker Martyr That Was Hanged on Boston Common, June 1, 1660* (Providence: Preston and Rounds, 1896).

6. Francis J. Bremer and Tom Webster, eds., *Puritans and Puritanism in Europe and America: A Comprehensive Encyclopedia.* 2 vols. (Santa Barbara, CA: ABC-CLIO, Inc., 2006).

7. Earl Warren, *A Republic, If You Can Keep It* (Chicago: Quadrangle Books, 1972).

8. Constitution of the United States, Amendment I (ratified in 1791).

9. *Cantwell v. Connecticut,* 310 U.S. 296, 60 S. Ct. 900 (1940).

10. Constitution of the United States, Amendment XIV (ratified in 1868).

11. See note to Exodus 7:8–11:10, *New Oxford Annotated Bible (New Revised Standard Version with the Apocrypha)* copyright © 1989 by the Division of Christian Education of the National Council of the Churches of Christ in the U.S.A., 92.

12. Ibid., 709.

13. See article by Theodore Walker, Jr., "Theological Resources for a Black Neoclassical Social Ethics," *Black Theology: A Documentary History,* Vol. Two (Maryknoll, NY: Orbis Books, 1993), 37–38.

14. Martin Luther King, Jr., "Letter from a Birmingham Jail," as reprinted in *A Testament of Hope: The Essential Writings of Martin Luther King, Jr.* James Melvin Washington, ed. (New York: Harper & Row, 1986), 300.

15. Excerpt of email message received November 5, 2015 from Rev. Daniel Buford, Minister of Justice, Allen Temple Baptist Church, Oakland, California (footnotes added). Reprinted with permission.

16. See www.religionnews.com/2015/06/05/ugandan-priest-lgbt-people-fleeing-kenya-avoid-rampant-discimination/, accessed January 9, 2017.

17. See http://thinkprogress.org/world/2015/05/08/3657028/actual-religious-persecution-looks-like-china/, accessed January 9, 2017.

18. See www.patheos.com/blogs/formerlyfundie/when-theology-is-so-pro-israel-that-it-becomes-anti-christian/, accessed January 9, 2017.

19. See www.rt.com/news/un-israel-west-bank-demolition-090/, accessed January 9, 2017.

20. Address of Marvin A. McMickle to Baptist Joint Committee Luncheon, delivered June 19, 2015 in Dallas, Texas.

CHAPTER 4

Rethinking Repentance and Reconciliation[1]

> Zacchaeus stood there and said to the Lord, "Look, half
> of my possessions, Lord, I will give to the poor; and if I
> have defrauded anyone of anything, I will pay back four
> times as much." Then Jesus said to him, "Today salvation
> has come to this house, because he too is a son of
> Abraham . . ."—Luke 19:8-9

The major religions of the world agree that the practice of repentance
is an essential aspect of right fellowship with the Divine and others.
Biblical Hebrew expresses the idea of repentance by two verbs: *shuv* (to
return) and *nacham* (to feel sorrow). The New Testament uses the
Greek word *metanoia,* a compound word that joins the preposition
"meta" (after, with) with the verb "noeo" (to perceive, to think, the
result of perceiving or observing), to convey the idea of afterthought,
often expressed as a change of mind and conduct. The Bible uses the
words *repent, repentance,* and *repented* more than a hundred times.

Throughout the Bible, repentance is expressed as a call for a radical
turn from one way of life to another because of the relationship one has
with God. In that sense, repentance is more than sorrow or regret. It is
conversion from self-worship, self-love, self-trust, and self-righteousness to God-worship, God-love, God-trust, and righteousness according to God.

Repentance begins with admitting guilt for committing a wrong
against God and others (whether by commission or omission)—meaning confession. Beyond that, Scripture shows that repentance involves
turning away from the wrongful act or practice. Where the wrongful
act or practice is against others, repentance requires attempting to

make restitution for the wrong done and any injury caused by it or otherwise acting to reverse the harmful effects of the wrong or omission.

Baptists and other evangelicals interpret the Bible, in fact all of life, through the life and ministry of Jesus Christ. Jesus, like the other Hebrew prophets who lived before him, confronted the people of his time and place concerning the need for repentance. Mark's Gospel reports that "after John was arrested, Jesus came to Galilee, proclaiming the good news of God, and saying: 'The time is fulfilled, and the kingdom of God has come near; repent, and believe in the good news'" (Mark 1:14-15; see also Matthew 4:12-17; Luke 4:14-15). The idea of repentance for Jesus—as for the Hebrew prophets before him—involved rejecting idolatry of self and turning to (embracing) God's vision about how we relate to God and others.

Repentance for Jesus and the Hebrew prophets is not optional, morally or ethically. *Repentance is an ethical imperative.* Any notion of human salvation that omits or disregards the ethical imperative of repentance is inconsistent with the gospel of Jesus.

The entire process of repentance is part and parcel of the divine undertaking of salvation. At its essence, salvation involves the process by which humanity is reconciled back to God in faithful love. Like everything else in salvation, repentance is a gift from God that we either accept or reject by faith. We do not repent on our own. Repentance is God-inspired, God-focused, and must be God-purposed. In repentance, humans embrace the grace of God to confess, confront, and turn from idolatry of self and to be people of divine love, justice, truth, and hope.

But the grace of God that makes repentance possible—that makes repentance morally and ethically required—also impels us to perceive that sin produces estrangement. Sin causes us to be estranged from God, our Creator. At the same time sin causes us to be estranged from ourselves, other persons, and the rest of creation. Through repentance, we are impelled to turn from the ethics of chaos, estrangement, and self-righteousness and embrace reconciliation and community.

Repentance is a faithful response to prophetic protest

The Bible also reveals that persons and societies are called to repentance by prophetic challenge, not internal impulse. In Genesis we read of God confronting Adam and Eve following the Fall, and God confronting Cain after the murder of Abel. In Exodus Moses is the prophetic agent sent by God to confront the Egyptian empire with the repentance imperative concerning oppression of the Hebrew population (see Exodus 3:1-10).

The prophetic call to repentance is always an act of protest. It is an observation and objection that the way we live violates the Great Commandment that we love God with our whole being and love others as ourselves. Somehow, people are inspired to recognize that people are not living as God would have us live, meaning that our relationships are not right with God and one another, whether because of actions we take or duties we neglect. Somehow, the Spirit of God inspires people with insight about love, truth, and justice (righteousness). Somehow, those inspired people are then impelled to protest conditions and situations that violate the love, truth, and justice of God. Without that protest, idolatry of self prevents us from recognizing our sinfulness and confronting the imperative for repentance. Faithful obedience to the life and lordship of Jesus necessarily, therefore, involves obeying this call to be a person of prophetic protest.

Repentance does not begin with us. Repentance begins with God, whose love, truth, and justice define the meaning of right and wrong, good and evil, healthful and harmful, just and unjust. God inspires people to see situations and relationships from the divine perspective. Then God commissions those inspired people to become prophetic protestors with God for love, justice, and truth and to confront persons and societies to confess sinfulness, return to God, and restore what has been harmed because of sin.

There is no repentance, personally or societally, without the disturbance of that subversive protest, subversive in that it asserts a different and countercultural version about life, love, truth, and justice from what is the dominant narrative. God is literally Protestor in Chief concerning our actions and attitudes that violate divine love, truth, and justice. God summons prophetic protestors to proclaim God's demand that we live according to divine love, truth, and justice and to protest our failure and refusal to do so.

And in repentance, we join God in protesting our transgressions and derelictions. We not only agree with God that our transgressions and derelictions are wrong and harmful. We agree to turn back toward God in repentance to protest our sinfulness, and in repentance turn away from that sinfulness and toward God. With God's help we become protestors of our ways. We not only agree with God that our ways require prophetic protest. In repentance we also become God's people of protest, prophetic and subversive agents of divine love, truth, and justice. We never become repentant people without somehow becoming prophetic people about God's love, truth, and righteousness (justice).

Thus, the Hebrew prophets, John the Baptist, Jesus, and the people who followed Jesus were prophetic subversives of repentance. They were markedly and intentionally inspired to view life and living from the radically different perspective of divine love, truth, and justice. That inspiration caused Moses to confront Egyptian unjust treatment of Hebrew workers (see Exodus 3:1–5:3). Nathan was inspired to protest to David about misusing personal and political power in his relationships with Bathsheba and Uriah (see 2 Samuel 11:1–12:13). Isaiah, Amos, Micah, Jeremiah, and Ezekiel were inspired to protest the ways that social, political, commercial, and other forms of power were abused to oppress widows, children, immigrants, workers, the weak, and people who were poor (see Isaiah 1:10-23; Amos 5:4-24; Micah 3, 6:1-15, 7:17; Jeremiah 5:20-31; Ezekiel 33:1-20). Jesus was inspired by the Holy Spirit to protest the ways power was abused by religious authorities to oppress rather than to liberate, to rupture fellowship rather than nurture reconciliation, and to benefit the wealthy while disregarding the plight of suffering people (see Matthew 23:13-39; 25:31-46).

By contrast, evangelicals who profess to follow Jesus have historically been reluctant to engage in prophetic protest about societal injustices.

The failure of most evangelical pastors, lay leaders, religious educators, and denominational leaders to challenge Donald Trump's repeated utterances of anti-immigrant rhetoric during the 2016 presidential election season was one of several glaring examples of that reluctance.

Evangelical views about repentance and injustice

Baptists and other evangelical followers of Jesus have always viewed repentance as an inseparable aspect of the grace of God leading to salvation. We speak about repentance as a change of heart inspired by the Holy Spirit and conviction that our sin offends God and violates the conditions by which we are in right relationship with God and others. Baptists have held this view across the centuries and wherever Baptists have created fellowships of believers in the gospel of Jesus. Yet in doing so, Baptists and other followers of Jesus have stressed repentance as an aspect of personal piety, not an ethical imperative for doing justice. We speak, write, preach, and sing about repentance as part of one's personal relationship with God. But we rarely speak of repentance as necessary for healing broken relationships between people who abuse power and others victimized by abuses of power. This pietistic concept of repentance, however sincerely it may be held and practiced, does not square with the way repentance is presented in Scripture.

In other words, there is a marked disconnect between the biblical approach to repentance and the way most Christian bodies, including Baptist denominations and fellowships, have understood and practiced repentance. The Hebrew writings and the New Testament Gospels demonstrate that repentance always requires acts of restitution and restoration that nurture reconciliation and reunion.

In the Torah, the sin offering was presented to atone for sin based on acknowledgment of *guilt*, while the trespass offering was presented to atone for sin based on acknowledgment of *injury*. The trespass offering ritual in the Torah reminds us that sin against others always involves more than personal guilt. Sin also causes damage, harm, and injury to relationships with others. That damage, harm, and injury is

49

not atoned for without voluntary and intentional conduct to repair what has been harmed, damaged, or injured. We never repair the harm, damage, or injury—or undo the oppression of sin against others—by merely making an apology.

Acknowledging guilt is important. But acknowledging guilt does not restore what has been wrongfully taken. Acknowledging guilt does not rebuild what has been destroyed. Acknowledging guilt does not heal what has been wounded. We need more than a confession of guilt. The work of healing what has been wounded, righting what has been wronged, and restoring what has been stolen or destroyed requires doing justice. It requires the ethics of restitution, reparation, restoration, and reconciliation. Until we do these things, we have not engaged in biblical repentance, no matter what else we may have accomplished.

Baptists have emphasized the need to acknowledge guilt and remorse concerning sin, but we have consistently shown less enthusiasm about acknowledging the way sin injures, harms, and oppresses others. We often speak of the need for confession but resist—and some may even say *resent*—the biblical mandates for restitution, reparation, and restoration that are the foundation for reconciliation, meaning restoration of community.

Allow me to refer to a famous example from recent memory that occurred in 1995. During the 150th anniversary of the Southern Baptist Convention, messengers in Atlanta, Georgia, adopted an eloquent resolution on racial reconciliation. The resolution admits that slavery played a role in the formation of the Southern Baptist Convention. It admits that Southern Baptists "defended the right to own slaves, and either participated in, supported, or acquiesced in the particularly inhumane nature of American slavery." The resolution also admits that Southern Baptists "later . . . failed, in many cases to support, and in some cases opposed, legitimate initiatives to secure the civil rights of African Americans."

The resolution goes on to admit that racism "has led to discrimination, oppression, injustice, and violence . . . throughout the history of our nation." It laments that racism and "historic acts of evil such as slavery from which we continue to reap a bitter harvest . . . [have] separated us from our African American brothers and sisters." Thus, the resolution resolves to apologize to "all African Americans for condoning and/or perpetuating individual and systemic racism in our lifetime; and we genuinely repent of racism of which we have been guilty, whether consciously (citing Psalm 19:13) or unconsciously (citing Leviticus 4:27)."

I do not question the sincerity of the messengers in Atlanta who adopted that eloquent expression of collective guilt and remorse for racism, slavery, discrimination, and other oppression related to racism toward African Americans. Yet it is striking that the messengers resolved to "ask forgiveness from our African American brothers and sisters, acknowledging *that our own healing is at stake*" [emphasis added]. The resolution is conspicuously, and I might add suspiciously, silent about healing the damage, injury, and harm suffered by African Americans because of more than 250 years of slavery, another century of legalized segregation, and continued systemic practices and policies that are the pernicious legacy of that tragic history.

Respectfully, let us contrast that resolution with an experience from the life of Jesus that South African theologian Allan Aubrey Boesak addressed in the book titled *Radical Reconciliation: Beyond Political Pietism and Christian Quietism*, which Boesak coauthored with Curtiss Paul DeYoung.[2] Boesak draws on the story of Zacchaeus (Luke 19:1-9), the chief tax collector who lived in Jericho and was both extremely rich and hated because he superintended an oppressive tax-collection regime.

Zacchaeus not only received a stipend from the Roman authorities for collecting taxes, he also took a percentage of whatever his agents collected. If tax collectors in general were hated by the people, Zacchaeus, as chief tax collector, was hated most of all. Boesak remarks that Zacchaeus chose a tree perch for a chance to see Jesus not merely because he was short in stature but because being in a tree was the safest spot for him, given how much he was hated and alienated from the people oppressed because of the tax-collection enterprise he operated for the Roman government.

As we know, Jesus invited himself to dinner at the home of Zacchaeus, that notoriously oppressive and wealthy man. We have no transcript of their dinner conversation, but whatever transpired between Jesus and Zacchaeus inspired the chief tax collector to divest himself of half his wealth and add that "if I have defrauded anyone of anything I will pay back four times as much" (Luke 19:8). Boesak points to Zacchaeus as instructive about ten things that are required to make repentance and reconciliation genuine, workable, and sustainable.

First, Zacchaeus acknowledged his personal complicity in and benefit from a system of oppressing others. Boesak writes that Zacchaeus did not "try and defend himself by arguing that he had to make a living, that this was merely his job, or that he had a family to look after. He knew that he unjustly benefited from oppression and suffering."[3]

Second, reconciliation requires both remorse and acknowledging that the victim of oppression has a right to righteous anger. Boesak adds that "my victim also has a right to restitution—it has nothing to do with my magnanimity, it is all about justice. It is acknowledging my victim's pain as a result of what I have done, and making it right with acts of justice."[4]

Third, reconciliation is not merely spiritual but produces restitution—meaning real and tangible gains for victims of oppression. Pledging to give half of his possessions to the poor and pay back four times whatever he had stolen was not a symbolic gesture. It was an act of restitution required in order make repentance result in justice, rather than merely an assuagement of guilt. Restitution is always substantive, never symbolic. According to Boesak, "Without restitution, reconciliation is not possible."[5] Otherwise, we are proponents of the cheap grace that Dietrich Bonhoeffer debunked so persuasively in *The Cost of Discipleship*.

Fourth, "there can be no reconciliation without equality."[6] By divesting himself of half his wealth and restoring four times whatever he had stolen from what remained, Zacchaeus removed himself from the exclusive club of the wealthy in Jericho and became a man of the people. Repentance results in reconciliation when we divest ourselves of unjustly obtained privilege and power.

Fifth, repentance and reconciliation involves more than restoring our broken relationship with God but is also about repairing and restoring broken relationships with others. Zacchaeus didn't merely make a private confession to Jesus that he was wrong. He demonstrated his genuine remorse and conversion by making a public commitment to restitution because he recognized that it was necessary to accomplish justice.[7]

Sixth, Zacchaeus didn't treat his sin as between himself and God. Unlike David, who said in Psalm 51:4, "Against you, you alone, have I sinned," thereby limiting his notion of repentance to a personal relationship with God while expressing no concern for the impact of his sin on Bathsheba and Uriah, Zacchaeus made a public expression of remorse and shame backed by his commitment to restitution and restoration to people harmed by his sin.[8]

Seventh, Boesak points out that when reconciliation (which is the end result of repentance) involves "uncovering the sin, showing remorse, making restitution, and restoring relationships with deeds of compassionate justice, then, and only then, is reconciliation complete, right, sustainable, and radical, because it becomes transformational. That is its salvific power."[9] We are not called to repentance in order to merely experience relief from guilt. The divine imperative of repentance works to transform us from self-worshipping beings into God-glorifying agents of love, truth, and justice.

Eighth, genuine reconciliation results not only in personal salvation but also "brings salvation for Zacchaeus *and his house.*" Because of the commitment to repentance and restitution that Zacchaeus demonstrated by divesting himself of half of his wealth (wealth derived because Zacchaeus benefited from systemic oppression), Zacchaeus's household, meaning his entire circle of intimate family relationships, was "released from the generational curse of guilt and shame that comes with exploitative, systemic relationships."[10]

Ninth, Boesak contends that repentance and reconciliation for Zacchaeus—the result of his experience with Jesus—impelled

Zacchaeus to *confront* his life of oppression and self-aggrandizement as a functionary of Roman imperialism and *convert* to a value system focused on divine justice rather than imperial dictates and personal perks. As Boesak puts it, "Zacchaeus switched sides."[11] I think this is what Dr. Martin Luther King Jr. meant when he spoke of the need to embrace what he called a "radical revolution of values" in the sermon he delivered at Riverside Church to announce his opposition to the US war in Southeast Asia on April 4, 1967. Repentance is more than personal salvation, privilege, and relief from guilt. It involves changing sides and joining God in creating what King and Howard Thurman before him called "the Beloved Community."

Tenth, and finally, Boesak affirms that reconciliation—which requires repentance—produces a new identity. Repentance changed Zacchaeus from being known as "a chief tax collector" to being "a son of Abraham."[12] Repentance involves the kind of faith that not only changes how we feel but also changes us intrinsically, so that we are always becoming people of divine love, truth, and justice.

Jesus shows us through the encounter with Zacchaeus that biblical repentance always involves a great deal more than making an apology. Biblical repentance demands action to restore fellowship, heal injuries, and provide recompense for harms that cause unwarranted suffering to others. Repentance requires that the wrongdoer acknowledge the holy anger of victims about what they have suffered, not insist that victims swallow that anger to spare the beneficiaries of oppression from discomfort and inconvenience.

What is conspicuously and suspiciously missing from the 1995 resolution adopted by the Southern Baptist Convention to apologize for slavery, racism, and discrimination is any commitment like that shown by Zacchaeus to make restitution to the historical victims of racism, slavery, and discrimination. Instead, the resolution entreats African Americans for forgiveness by affirming that "our own healing is at stake." No commitment is affirmed, let alone pledged, to do the healing work of justice for people whose ancestors were enslaved, dehumanized, defrauded, terrorized, and marginalized—and who continue to suffer from that colossal violation of divine love, truth, and justice.

Respectfully, I contend that the 1995 resolution exposes a fundamental misunderstanding about and misrepresentation of what the gospel of Jesus teaches about repentance and reconciliation. If we are serious about racial reconciliation as followers of the Jesus who encountered Zacchaeus, Baptists and any other followers of Jesus must confront and confess the glaring ethical difference between merely apologizing for historical oppression and correcting the consequences of that oppression through restitution leading to reconciliation. Repentance, like grace, is costly, not cheap. When Baptists, who profess to believe in the authority of Scripture and the lordship of Jesus, treat repentance as was shown by the 1995 Atlanta resolution concerning racism, slavery, and discrimination, we are merely being apologetic, not repentant.

In making this observation I do not denounce the 1995 resolution as insincere. However sincere it may be, it is clearly a far cry from what Jesus showed repentance to involve through the example of Zacchaeus. According to that example, the litmus test for repentant sincerity is not defined by how conspicuously one apologizes for transgressions and derelictions that oppress others. It is whether our apology is accompanied by actions that heal wounds, confront and eliminate inequality, and honor the righteous anger of the oppressed. Without those things, an apology amounts to mere rhetoric.

Justice is always much more than a rhetorical exercise. Perhaps that is one reason Baptists are not considered prophetic when it comes to social justice concerns involving racism, sexism, classism, imperialism, militarism, techno-centrism, and xenophobia. For all its eloquent sincerity, the 1995 resolution represents to Baptists, and to the wider world, that the largest body of Baptists considers repentance to mean little more than apologizing for wrongfulness and doing no more than what is convenient.

In June 2014 *The Atlantic* magazine published a compelling article by Ta-Nehesi Coates that began with this passage from Deuteronomy 15:12-15:

If a member of your community, whether a Hebrew man or a Hebrew woman, is sold to you and works for you six years, in the seventh year you shall set that person free. And when you send a male slave out from you a free person, you shall not send him out empty-handed. Provide liberally out of your flock, your threshing floor, and your wine press, thus giving to him some of the bounty with which the LORD your God has blessed you. Remember that you were a slave in the land of Egypt, and the LORD your God redeemed you; for this reason, I lay this command upon you today.

Coates opened his article, titled "The Case for Reparations," with that passage. It is remarkable that a journalist of a secular magazine has been more prophetically forthright about the essential relationship between reparations and social justice, using the same Bible that Baptists profess to be authoritative for our faith and practice, than clergy, laypersons, congregations, denominations, and educational institutions who profess to be followers of Jesus.

Until we are prepared to become more than apologists concerning historical transgressions and derelictions, our appeals about repentance to the rest of the world will ring hollow. We will enable the world to embrace a "cheap grace" perspective about repentance and salvation that runs contrary to the entire record of Scripture, including the teachings and example of Jesus.

At best, we will be weak witnesses to the transforming and salvific work of repentance in a world ravaged by racism, sexism, classism, militarism, imperialism, techno-centrism, and xenophobia. At worst, we will be considered hypocrites. If the people who follow Jesus are unwilling to practice biblical repentance, as displayed by Zacchaeus, concerning past and continuing harms, we should not be surprised when the rest of the world refuses to do so and disregards what we say, sing, and preach concerning the relationship between repentance, salvation, and reconciliation.

In sum, the world needs to see us living as prophetic witnesses who proclaim and incarnate the salvation ethic of repentance. God calls us, through Jesus Christ and the Holy Spirit, to embrace the radical, revolutionary, and subversive repentance that Jesus revealed for us through his encounter with Zacchaeus.

But not only is the world waiting for evangelical followers of Jesus to confront that ethical imperative in our personal, congregational, associational, and wider relationships and witness. God is waiting and hoping that we will live as if we understand what Jesus, John the Baptist, the other Hebrew prophets, and the rest of Scripture have revealed about the transforming and reconciling power of repentance for God's sin-scarred and broken humanity and God's wounded creation.

Discussion and Reflection Questions

1. Have you understood repentance to be a form of prophetic witness? If repentance is not a form of prophetic witness, how does repentance avoid becoming merely a matter of personal piety?

2. When have you been part of faith communities, congregations, or other groups that viewed repentance as a requirement for authentic justice and peace?

3. What do you think about how Dr. Allan A. Boesak links repentance to reconciliation in his discussion about the interaction between Jesus and Zacchaeus?

4. If the 1995 Southern Baptist Convention resolution on slavery was not true repentance, what was its redemptive power for the endorsers and for their relationship with descendants of slaves? What was its prophetic witness and effectiveness concerning US racism?

Notes

1. The views expressed in this chapter were first shared on March 23, 2015 during the 2015 T. B. Maston Lectures in Christian Ethics presented by Logsdon Seminary and Hardin-Simmons University at Abilene, Texas. I thank Bill Jones (Chair of the Board of Trustees for the T. B. Maston Foundation for Christian Ethics), Dean Don Williford of Logsdon Seminary, Dr. Larry Baker, Dr. Ray Higgins (Coordinator, Cooperative Baptist Fellowship of Arkansas), and Dr. Emmanuel McCall of McAfee School of Theology (Decatur, Georgia) for making it possible for me to share my thoughts about repentance and reconciliation in a lecture titled "Repentance,

Reconciliation, and Baptists—A Retrospective and Lessons from Our History." This chapter is a modified version of that lecture. The following day I delivered remarks titled "Repentance, Reconciliation, and Baptists—Re-Imagining and Embracing the Subversive Gospel of Jesus in the 21st Century." A modified version of that lecture appears in the next chapter of this book.

2. Allan Aubrey Boesak and Curtiss Paul DeYoung, *Radical Reconciliation: Beyond Political Pietism and Christian Quietism* (Maryknoll, New York: Orbis Books, 2012), 68.

3. Ibid.

4. Ibid.

5. Ibid.

6. Ibid.

7. Ibid., 69.

8. Ibid.

9. Ibid., 70.

10. Ibid., 71.

11. Ibid.

12. Ibid., 73.

CHAPTER 5

Re-Imagining and Embracing the Subversive Gospel of Jesus in the Twenty-First Century[1]

The way of peace they do not know,
and there is no justice in their paths.
Their roads they have made crooked;
no one who walks in them knows peace.
Therefore justice is far from us,
and righteousness does not reach us;
we wait for light, and lo! there is darkness;
and for brightness, but we walk in gloom. . . .
We wait for justice, but there is none;
for salvation, but it is far from us. —Isaiah 59:8-11

A year to the day before he was assassinated, Dr. Martin Luther King Jr., a Baptist pastor, publicly defined the war in Vietnam as a civil rights issue in his address of April 4, 1967 titled "Beyond Vietnam: A Time to Break Silence." Speaking to a meeting of Clergy and Laity Concerned about Vietnam at Riverside Church in New York City, Dr. King uttered the following prescient statement.

I am convinced that if we are to get on the right side of the world revolution, we as a nation must undergo a radical revolution of values. We must rapidly begin the shift from a "thing-oriented" society to a "person-oriented" society. When machines and computers, profit motives and property rights are considered more important than people, the giant triplets of racism, materialism, and militarism are incapable of being conquered.

A true revolution of values will soon cause us to question the fairness and justice of many of our past and present policies . . . There is nothing, except a tragic death wish, to prevent us from reordering our priorities, so that the pursuit of peace will take precedence over the pursuit of war.[2]

Public reaction to King's message was swift and hostile. A number of editorial writers attacked him for connecting Vietnam to the civil rights movement. The *New York Times* issued an editorial claiming that King had damaged the peace movement as well as the civil rights movement. *Life* magazine assailed the speech as "demagogic slander that sounded like a script for Radio Hanoi." The *Pittsburgh Courier*, an African American publication, charged King with "tragically misleading" black people. And at the White House, President Lyndon Johnson was quoted as saying, "What is that goddamned nigger preacher doing to me? We gave him the Civil Rights Act of 1964, we gave him the Voting Rights Act of 1965, we gave him the War on Poverty. What more does he want?"[3]

Dr. King was assassinated in Memphis, Tennessee, a year after he delivered this speech, written by Dr. Vincent Harding. Despite the hostile reaction to the speech, Martin King and Vincent Harding never disavowed it. But Dr. Harding, who passed away in 2014, always believed the speech was the reason King was murdered. "It was precisely one year to the day after this speech that that bullet which had been chasing him for a long time finally caught up with him," Dr. Harding said in a 2010 interview. "And I am convinced that that bullet had something to do with that speech. And over the years, that's been quite a struggle for me."[4]

Nine years after his death, Dr. King was posthumously awarded the Presidential Medal of Freedom by another Baptist from Georgia, President Jimmy Carter. A federal holiday has been established to honor his birthday. His statue has been erected in Washington, DC. Numerous cities and towns have renamed major traffic arteries for him, and he is revered throughout the world as one of the most prophetic souls of the twentieth century, if not the modern era. When President Barack Obama took the oath of office to begin his second term, he placed his hand on a Bible that belonged to Dr. King and alluded to him during his inaugural address.

Yet the veneration of Dr. King has not included any significant or serious effort by US policymakers, social commentators, and moral leaders—including Baptist and other evangelical clergy, laity, associations, denominations, and educational institutions—to embrace the "radical revolution of values" King called for in "Beyond Vietnam: A Time to Break Silence". The "giant triplets" of racism, militarism, and materialism have not been confronted. The US currently devotes more of its budget to national defense and homeland security than to educating children, fighting disease, feeding the hungry, and alleviating poverty.

We may never learn the true financial cost of the tragic military misadventure known as the war in Iraq. As the tenth anniversary of the war in Iraq approached, Reuters reported on a study by a team of academicians that tallied the cost of the war at $1.7 trillion, a figure that did not include $490 billion owed to Iraqi war veterans for disability benefits. The study projected that expenses related to the war in Iraq could grow to more than $6 trillion over the next four decades.[5]

At the same time that US leaders—including Baptist and other religious leaders—venerate King's memory, they have ignored or rejected his call for the United States to use its wealth and prestige to lead the world in a radical revolution of values that rejects war as the preferred means of resolving differences. President Barack Obama could not have been guided by the vision of the Baptist preacher whose Bible he used for his second inauguration. Although President Obama could not persuade US officials and global allies to embrace a military response to Syria the way President George W. Bush did concerning Iraq, US militarism continues to cast an ominous cloud over the world and hinder efforts to address glaring problems at home.

Dr. Jonathan Tran's 2012 essay about the war policies of the Obama administration reminds us that President Obama has articulated what Tran termed "a theology of war."[6] It is more than sadly ironic that the first African American to hold the office of President of the United States endorsed a policy of killing American citizens by using armed drones. The militarism King criticized is also evident in the virulent response by President Obama and other US leaders to the disclosures by Edward Snowden that the United States engaged in wholesale spying on American citizens and others throughout the world, including the leaders of nations considered its allies.

Forty-four years after Dr. King was murdered by a gunman, the nation witnessed the massacre of twenty children and six adult staff members of Sandy Hook Elementary School in Newtown, Connecticut, by a gunman who had already killed his mother and later killed himself. The militarism that drives US global policy seems to have turned on our own children. The response to the Sandy Hook massacre has not been, however, to confront the giant of militarism. Firearm manufacturers and their lobbyists, like defense contractors and their lobbyists, now hold more influence than ever before.

Sadly, devotion to corporate profit-making continues to hamstring efforts to make our society and the world safe. Thus, militarism has joined forces with materialism so much that American schools run the serious risk of becoming fortresses. We somehow are blind to the stark moral and ethical contradiction of singing "Let There Be Peace on Earth" while arming school teachers and cheering people who openly brandish handguns.

The moral and ethical disconnect between the rhetoric used to venerate Dr. King and the persistence of entrenched racism in American life continues to afflict us. Policymakers refuse to acknowledge the plain truth that the "law and order" and "war on drugs" mantras used by every US president since Lyndon Johnson have actually produced mass incarceration of millions of people who are disproportionately persons of color. Thanks to the not-always-covert racism of "law and order" and "war on drugs" enthusiasts, more black people were politically and socially disenfranchised in the United States in 2015 than were enslaved in 1850, ten years before the Civil War began—a fact that Professor Michelle Alexander forcefully presented in her

2010 book titled *The New Jim Crow: Mass Incarceration in the Age of Color-Blindness.*[7]

Oppressive law-enforcement policies that gave rise to civil unrest during Dr. King's lifetime still operate against people who are black and brown. Years after President Obama and Attorney General Eric Holder became the first black persons to hold their respective offices, the terrorism of racial profiling was as prevalent as when Dr. King was assassinated, if not more so.

Insensitivity to the insidious racism that poisoned the United States when Dr. King was killed has not changed. Trayvon Martin,[8] Oscar Grant,[9] and Amadou Diallo,[10] like Martin Luther King Jr., were black men shot to death by people who claimed the moral and legal right to take their lives. The racism and militarism Dr. King deplored in 1967 were major factors in the August 9, 2014 death of Michael Brown Jr., an eighteen-year-old unarmed black teenager shot to death by Darren Wilson, formerly of the Ferguson, Missouri Police Department.[11] That racism and militarism also accounted for the killing of Eric Garner, who was choked to death on July 23, 2014 by Daniel Pantaleo while other New York Police Department officers pressed their knees on Garner's torso despite his repeated statement, "I can't breathe!"[12] Plainly, the United States has not become more informed about or responsive to racial injustice since Dr. King died. We have simply militarized the injustice in brazen ways.

We have not confronted or corralled the giant triplets of militarism, materialism, and racism. Rather, we have added sexism (including homophobia), classism, techno-centrism, and xenophobia to the mix. The triplets are now septuplets!

The painful truth is that political, commercial, and even religious leaders are comfortable bestowing platitudes on Dr. King's life and ministry while actively and deliberately disregarding his warnings and call for repentance. Our leaders play on (I say they pimp) Dr. King's moral authority for their own benefit at every opportunity. However, they question the relevancy of his teachings and warnings for our time.

Such contradictory behavior amounts to what I call "re-assassination" of Dr. King. King's ministry and message is being re-murdered by drone warfare, NSA surveillance, a militarized law-enforcement culture, and our support for regimes that use military force to oppress minority populations in this society and elsewhere in the world (militarism), as well as by the half-truths and outright falsehoods uttered to defend those actions.

Dr. King is re-murdered by fiscal policies that promote the corporate interests of investment bankers over the lives and fortunes of workers, homeowners, retirees, and needy people (materialism).

King's dedication to attack and eliminate the causes of systemic poverty is currently being re-assassinated by policies that widen the glaring income inequality between the super-wealthy and the poor (classism).

King's righteous indignation against injustice is murdered by proponents of the so-called "prosperity gospel" and those who use religion as a weapon to deny civil rights to people who are lesbian, gay, bisexual, transgender, poor, immigrants, women, or otherwise vulnerable (racism, sexism, and xenophobia).

King's call for a radical revolution of values is murdered when we profess to honor his memory while bowing to the techno-centrism responsible for poisoning community aquifers through fracking for natural gas.

When we honestly assess the mood and conduct of US leaders and the public-at-large—including Baptist and other religious leaders—since Dr. King was assassinated in Memphis, it becomes clear that we have not chosen to embrace the "radical revolution of values" Dr. King articulated. We have not weakened the giant triplets of racism, militarism, and materialism. We have nourished, bred, and multiplied them. Religious leaders such as Rev. Dr. Jeremiah Wright Jr. who have followed Dr. King's model of prophetic criticism and congregational leadership have been rejected and condemned in much the same way that President Johnson responded to Dr. King.

Dr. King was correct when he observed in his April 4, 1967 adddress that "there is nothing, except a tragic death wish, to prevent us from reordering our priorities." Sadly, we seem unable to realize that by rejecting his call to reorder our values and priorities—in other words, to engage in the biblical imperative of repentance—we not only "re-assassinate" King. By rejecting his values while pretending to venerate King as our greatest prophet, we also destroy ourselves and risk forfeiting any moral authority we claim as agents for peace, justice, and truth in the world. Sooner or later, people who feed a death wish find a way to destroy themselves.

Followers of Jesus have a moral and ethical obligation to re-imagine and embrace the subversive gospel of Jesus Christ in the prophetic way King did. Our pastors and Christian educators must lead the way. Our congregations, associations, state conventions, and other fellowships must lovingly and honestly embrace our calling from God to be prophetic agents of divine love, truth, and justice about the wickedness of the septuplets: racism, sexism, materialism, classism, militarism, techno-centrism, and xenophobia.

I am periodically moved to revisit Ezekiel 2:1-7 and be reminded of what God has called me to be and do. I invite you to also ponder our ministry efforts as scholars, students, pastors, and denominational leaders from that perspective:

> He said to me: "O mortal, stand up on your feet, and I will speak with you." And when he spoke to me, a spirit entered into me and set me on my feet; and I heard him speaking to me. He said to me, "Mortal, I am sending you to the people of Israel, a nation of rebels who have rebelled against me; they and their ancestors have transgressed against me to this very day. The descendants are impudent and stubborn. I am sending you to them, and you shall say to them, 'Thus says the LORD God.' Whether they hear or refuse to hear (for they are a rebellious house), they shall know that there has been a prophet among them. And you, mortal, do not be afraid of them, and do not be afraid of their words, though briars and thorns surround you and you live among scorpions; do not be afraid of their words, and do not be dismayed by their looks, for they are a rebellious house. You shall speak my words to them, whether they hear or refuse to hear; for they are a rebellious house."

The issue now is whether we will be prophets of God's love, truth, and justice to the "rebellious house" where racism, sexism, materialism, militarism, classism, techno-centrism, and xenophobia rule with oppressive force. Are the men and women who answer to the name of Jesus prophets calling "the rebellious house" to repentance? Are we, like King, pleading with our society and world to embrace a "radical revolution of values" away from what now are giant septuplets of injustice? Are we nurturing this prophetic consciousness and determination in congregations, associations, and other Baptist fellowships? Or are we unwilling to take up the prophetic cross of Jesus Christ because we're afraid that doing so means we must somehow suffer and die?

We have been sent to a "rebellious house" to be prophets for God, not counselors to or cheerleaders for the principalities and powers responsible for racism, sexism, materialism, militarism, classism, techno-centrism, and xenophobia.

We are called by God to be prophets to the "rebellious house" of principalities and powers that believe in profit regardless of the cost to creation or the health and safety of workers and communities.

We are called by God to be prophets to the "rebellious house" where capitalism is worshipped above God and the mindset of Wal-Mart is preferred to the Spirit of Jesus.

Yet prophets are not only God's voices of holy protest to "the rebellious house." Prophets are God's agents of hope. To borrow from South African theologian Allan Boesak, I now ask if we dare to speak of hope in the face of the principalities and powers responsible for racism, materialism, militarism, sexism, classism, techno-centrism, and xenophobia.

Yes! We must dare to speak of hope, even while engaging in prophetic protest about the systemic causes of injustice and suffering, because of the gospel of Jesus.

We must dare to speak of hope, but only while confronting and suffering, with God, the wounds of racism, materialism, militarism, sexism, classism, techno-centrism, and xenophobia. Allan Boesak calls us to dare to speak of hope, but only if we speak of anger and courage—

what Augustine of Hippo called the beautiful daughters of hope. "Anger at the way things are, and courage to see that they do not remain the same."[13]

We must dare to speak of hope and struggle and grieve with God against the principalities and powers responsible for the giant septuplets.[14]

We must dare to speak of hope, but not without prophetically calling our society and the rest of the world to turn from our addiction to violence and war by embracing peace.[15]

We must dare to speak of hope, audaciously, despite the fragility of our faith.[16]

We must dare to speak of hope and dream, to borrow from the words of Nelson Mandela, "that there has emerged a cadre of leaders in my country and region, on my continent and in the world, which will not allow that any should be denied their freedom, as we were; that any should be turned into refugees, as we were; that any should be condemned to go hungry, as we were; that any should be stripped of their human dignity, as we were."[17]

We are prophets called by God to confront our "rebellious house" with the moral necessity and ethical imperative of repentance. But we are not doomsayers. We are prophets of the gospel of Jesus, a gospel that does not stop with Calvary and Good Friday.

We are prophets of the gospel of Jesus, a gospel that does not pretend to be blind about evil yet will not flinch when confronting it. We are prophets of Jesus, the Resurrected One.

We are prophets of resurrection hope! We are prophets of resurrection joy! We are prophets of the way-making and empire-shaking God! We are prophets of the extravagantly merciful God! We are prophets of hope because God loved us, saved us, and called us through the life of Jesus Christ.

We are prophets of hope. Shameless hope! Audacious fragile hope! Angry hope! Courageous hope! Wounded hope! Dreaming hope!

God has called us. God sends us. God is counting on us to make a prophetic and hopeful difference in God's world as followers of Jesus Christ by the power of the Holy Spirit.

Discussion Questions and Reflections

1. In what specific and intentional ways are you, like Dr. Martin Luther King Jr., pleading with our society and world to embrace a "radical revolution of values" against the giant septuplets of injustice (racism, sexism—including homophobia, materialism, imperialism, militarism, techno-centrism, and xenophobia)?

2. In what ways is Dr. King being "re-assassinated" in your community? Who are the agents and forces of that "re-assassination"?

3. How are you nurturing a prophetic consciousness and determination in your congregations, associations, and other fellowships and interactions?

4. What have you done in the past and what are you doing currently to demonstrate righteous anger, courage, and hope in the face of systemic injustice and its consequences?

Notes

1. The views expressed in this chapter are a modified version of my remarks originally titled "Repentance, Reconciliation, and Baptists—Re-imagining and Embracing the Subversive Gospel of Jesus in the 21st Century" and delivered at Hardin-Simmons University on March 24, 2015.

2. "Beyond Vietnam: A Time to Break Silence" is among the writings of Dr. King compiled by James Melvin Washington and published under the title *A Testament of Hope: The Essential Writings of Martin Luther King, Jr.* (San Francisco: Harper and Row, 1986).

3. For reactions to "Beyond Vietnam: A Time to Break Silence," see www.americanrhetoric.com/speeches/mlkatimetobreaksilence.htm.

4. See www.nytimes.com/2014/05/22/us/vincent-harding-civil-rights-author-and-associate-of-dr-king-dies-at-82.html?_r=0, accessed January 9, 2017.

5. See www.reuters.com/article/2013/03/14/us-iraq-war-anniversary-idUSBRE92D0PG20130314, accessed January 9, 2017.

6. Jonathan Tran, "Obama, War, and Christianity: The Audacity of Hope and the Violence of Peace," *Christian Ethics Today*, Spring 2012.

7. Michelle Alexander, *The New Jim Crow: Mass Incarceration in the Age of Color-Blindness* (New York: The New Press, 2010).

8. Trayvon Martin was a seventeen-year-old black male who was shot to death by George Zimmerman as Martin was returning to his father's residence from a convenience store in Sanford, Florida, the night of February 26, 2012. Zimmerman was acquitted by a jury on the charge of manslaughter.

9. Oscar Grant III was fatally shot in the back at point blank range by Bay Area

Rapid Transit (BART) police officer Johannes Mehserle during the early hours of New Year's Day of 2009 in Oakland, California. Mehserle was eventually convicted by a jury of involuntary manslaughter and served only two years in the Los Angeles County Jail, minus time served.

10. Amadou Diallo was a twenty-three-year-old Guinean immigrant who was shot and killed by four New York City Police officers who fired 41 bullets, 19 of which struck Diallo, outside his apartment in the Bronx. All four police officers were later acquitted of criminal charges related to Diallo's death.

11. See www.nytimes.com/interactive/2014/08/13/us/ferguson-missouri-town-under-siege-after-police-shooting.html?_r=0, accessed on January 9, 2017.

12. See 2017 www.theguardian.com/us-news/video/2014/dec/04/i-cant-breathe-eric-garner-chokehold-death-video, accessed January 9, 2017. Readers are cautioned that the video showing police officers pressing on Garner's torso while Daniel Pantaleo choked him despite his dying gasps about not being able to breathe is extremely difficult to view. Prophetic truth compels that followers of Jesus bear witness and express prophetic outrage about the injustice of Garner's treatment and death, not merely utter sympathetic apologies about it.

13. See Allan Aubrey Boesak, *Dare We Speak of Hope? Searching for a Language of Life in Faith and Politics* (Grand Rapids, MI: Eerdmans, 2014), chap. 2.

14. Ibid., chap. 3.

15. Ibid., chap. 4.

16. Ibid., chap. 5.

17. Nelson Mandela, quoted in *Dare We Speak of Hope?*, 146.

CHAPTER 6

Repentance and God's Subversive Ways

The Lord said, "Rise and anoint him; for this is the one."
Then Samuel took the horn of oil, and anointed him in the
presence of his brothers; and the spirit of the LORD came
mightily upon David from that day forward. —1 Samuel
16:12-13

In 1998 Dr. Spencer Johnson authored a remarkable little motivational
book titled *Who Moved My Cheese?* that was sort of a fable or parable. The book features two mice (Sniff and Scurry) and two "littlepeo-
ple" (Hem and Haw) who live in a maze and look for cheese. In the
book, cheese is a metaphor for success and contentment. The focus of
the story involves how we adjust to changes in our routines. What happens in us when the ways we have habitually functioned become different?

Traditional notions of leadership were turned upside down when
Samuel, a celebrated judge and prophet of Israel, was sent to find a suc-
cessor to King Saul among the sons of Jesse. Samuel learned that God
doesn't function the way we do when it comes to performing a talent
search. Samuel thought that Eliab, the tall and handsome eldest son of
Jesse, would certainly be God's choice—only to learn that he was
wrong. When none of the assembled sons of Jesse were found accept-
able, Samuel was forced to understand something else: Jesse didn't
summon one son, his youngest, to be interviewed.

The account includes this poignant exchange between Samuel and
Jesse in 1 Samuel 16:11: "Samuel said to Jesse, 'Are all your sons here?'

And he said, 'There remains the youngest, but he is keeping the sheep.' And Samuel said to Jesse, 'Send and bring him, for we will not sit down until he comes here.'"

There remains the youngest. Jesse didn't present the youngest of his sons for Samuel to interview. That shows our preference for seniority.

He is keeping the sheep. David is not only the youngest son, he is a herdsman of sheep. Sheep are smelly creatures, so it is safe to say that David was at a respectable distance from the place where his father and elder brothers were entertaining Samuel. David was a worker with livestock. His father didn't voluntarily invite the herdsman for what was an interview process for a public policy job.

Send and bring him here, for we will not sit down until he comes here. Samuel stood protocol on its head. He refused to begin the banquet without David. Everything was put on hold until David arrived. That involved waiting until someone found David (wherever he was leading the herd), waiting longer until David traveled from the herd to the house, and perhaps waiting even longer while David cleaned up to present himself for inspection. Samuel insisted that Jesse and the older sons, the privileged, wait until David (the youngest son who was unprivileged) arrived.

Samuel used his privilege as judge and prophet to empower the unprivileged and disfavored David. And Samuel was inspired by God to select David, over all his older brothers and against the preference of his father, as the next king of Israel. David went from being the least favored of his father's sons to become the favorite of God! God moved the cheese!

The gospel account of Jesus giving sight to a man blind since birth (John 9:1-41) presents more *Who Moved My Cheese?* lessons.

"Rabbi, who sinned, this man or his parents, that he was born blind?" (John 9:2). Jesus first had to contend with the traditional view of his disciples that blindness from birth was a divine punishment rather than a disability.

"He spat on the ground and made mud with the saliva and spread the mud on the man's eyes" (John 9:6). The therapy Jesus provided doesn't

fit our notions of respectability, to put it mildly. How much of our lives are restricted by conventional notions of what is "respectable"?

"This man is not from God, for he does not observe the Sabbath" (John 9:16). The response of some religious traditionalists to the now-sighted man was not joy about his deliverance but consternation that the Sabbath tradition had been violated by his liberation from blindness. Jesus, who certainly knew it was the Sabbath when he treated the blind man, was considered a moral threat.

"The man answered, 'If this man were not from God, he could do nothing.' They answered him, 'You were born entirely in sins, and are trying to teach us?' And they drove him out." This exchange at verses 33-34 is more "cheese-moving." The formerly blind man was the one who recognized Jesus as God's agent among them, while the religious experts were unable or unwilling to admit that truth.

"I came into this world for judgment so that those who do not see may see, and those who do see may become blind." With these words in John 9:39, Jesus summarized the subversive ways of God.

Rev. Glenn Jones (senior pastor of St. Paul's Presbyterian Church, Coliseum and La Brea, in Los Angeles) likes to say that "God works in mischievous ways." The Hebrew Testament account of how David, the youngest son of his father, Jesse, came to be anointed king of Israel, and John's account about how Jesus healed an unnamed man who had been born blind, prove that observation. They offer vivid examples of God subverting human customs, processes, and expectations.

God moves the cheese! And in doing so, God exposes our need to repent on so many levels.

God exposes how we tend to crave and worship privilege, status, and tradition.

God exposes how we disfavor and mistreat people based on what they do, who they are, or how life has affected them.

God exposes how we resent and abhor methods that are different or unconventional.

God exposes how we resist learning from people based on our sense of superiority. The religious people who eventually banished the man whom Jesus healed considered themselves morally superior to him sim-ply because they had been born with sight and he was born blind.

God is subversive! We are conservative. God is radical! We are reac-tionary. God is liberating! We tend to create and maintain systems that are oppressive. So the gospel of Jesus Christ constantly challenges us to repent from our addiction to privilege, tradition, status, and the falla-cies of "conventional wisdom."

Pope Francis offers a current example of the subversive ways of God. In early December 2013, he gave an "apostolic exhortation," an address calling for big changes in the Catholic Church, including rethinking long-held but antiquated customs. "I prefer a Church which is bruised, hurting and dirty because it has been out on the streets, rather than a Church which is unhealthy from being confined and from clinging to its own security," he stated. "I do not want a Church con-cerned with being at the center and then ends by being caught up in a web of obsessions and procedures." And in November of last year, Pope Francis issued an Apostolic Exhortation that condemned what he termed an "economy of exclusion" in these words:

> How can it be that it is not a news item when an elderly home-less person dies of exposure, but it is news when the stock mar-ket loses two points? . . . Some people continue to defend trickle-down theories which assume that economic growth . . . will . . . succeed in bringing about greater justice and inclusiveness. . . . To sustain a lifestyle which excludes others, or to sustain enthusiasm for that selfish ideal, a globalization of indifference has developed. Almost without being aware of it, we end up being incapable of feeling compassion at the outcry of the poor, weeping for other people's pain, and feeling a need to help them, as though all this were someone else's responsibility and not our own.[1]

This is subversive speech to people who worship at the altar of free-market capitalism. This is subversive speech to those who, like Jesse and his elder sons, are content to conduct their affairs without concern for those who are, like David, the disfavored. This is subversive speech to those who, like the people who criticized Jesus for healing the blind man, are more interested in maintaining their traditions than doing justice. Pope Francis is articulating the gospel of Jesus Christ and calling the world to repentance by asserting subversive truth.

The subversive truth of God demands our repentance because the subversive love of God demands it. The subversive love of God demands our repentance because the subversive justice of God demands it. The subversive justice of God demands our repentance because the subversive peace—prosperity and good health—of God demands it.

Let us, therefore, take up the "mischievous ways" of our subversive God. Let us condemn and call our world to throw off its blind faith in what Pope Francis correctly has called "the economy of exclusion." Let us turn away from the idolatry of money and privilege and status that defines our time. Let us, as followers of Jesus Christ, be agents of the subversive love, subversive justice, subversive truth, subversive hope, subversive peace, and subversive joy of God!

God will help us. Let us repent and take up this great subversive living to the glory of our subversive God.

Discussion and Reflection Questions

1. How does your life demonstrate the subversive ways of God? How has your living been true to prophetic examples in the Bible about how God has worked through others?

2. What are some present examples of God working in subversive ways to challenge and frustrate notions of empire, greed, self-worship, violence, and hate in your community?

3. How are you involving yourself with those efforts? If you aren't yet involved, when will you begin doing so? What will it require for that to happen?

4. How are you, like Jesse and Samuel, expecting God to work through traditional notions of privilege, power, and authority?

Notes

1. The full text of the English translation of the November 2013 Apostolic Exhortation can be found at www.vatican.va/holy_father/francesco/apost_exhorta
tions/documents/papa-francesco_esortazione-ap_20131124_evangeli
i-audium_en.html#I.%E2%80%82Some_challenges_of_today%E2%80%99s_
world, accessed January 9, 2017.

CHAPTER 7

Subversive Magi, the Gospel of Jesus, and Us

In the time of King Herod, after Jesus was born in Bethlehem of Judea, wise men from the East came to Jerusalem, asking, "Where is the child who has been born king of the Jews? For we observed his star at its rising, and have come to pay him homage." When King Herod heard this, he was frightened, and all Jersusalem with him; . . . Then Herod secretly called for the wise men and learned from them the exact time when the star had appeared. Then he sent them to Bethlehem, saying, "Go and search diligently for the child; and when you have found him, bring me word so that I may also go and pay him homage." . . . And having been warned in a dream not to return to Herod, they left for their own country by another road.
—Matthew 2:1-3,7-8,12

In December 2015, I took an immersion tour of Israel and Palestine as part of a twelve-person group.[1] Our experience, upon arriving at Ben Gurion International Airport in Tel Aviv, during our trip, and when departing led me to rethink what happened to the Magi who were looking for Jesus, what their visit meant, and their decision to return to their homeland without obtaining an exit visa from Herod the Great.

International travelers must pass through immigration and customs and obtain an "entry visa" when entering another country, so after our flight landed at Tel Aviv, everyone in our group was questioned about the purpose for our visit and how long we expected to visit. We were not allowed to proceed into Israel until Israeli immigration officials were satisfied with our responses. Only then was each person granted an entry visa, the document that authorized one's presence in Israel.[2]

When we departed the country several days later, immigration officials again questioned us. They demanded to know why we visited Israel, how long we were there, whether anyone gave us anything perishable or dangerous to transport from the country, and other routine inquiries. We were each given an "exit visa" only after the officials were satisfied with our responses.

We tend, and are tempted, to not consider such social, political, cultural, and other contextual factors when we read and interpret Scripture. Consider what we read in Matthew 2 about the visit of the Magi. Why do we sing "We Three Kings of Orient Are" when Matthew doesn't declare how many magi made the pilgrimage? Is it fair and honest, or simply sentimentally convenient, to believe that there were three magi because three gifts (gold, frankincense, and myrrh) were presented to Jesus?

We also tend to romanticize how King Herod the Great received the Magi. Recall that Herod (and the political and religious establishment he oversaw as a puppet ruler installed by the Roman Empire in Palestine) was "frightened" by the arrival of Magi from the East who came to pay homage to a child they said was "born king of the Jews." Perhaps we should consider Matthew's account of the reception of the Magi from the perspective of foreign travelers being interviewed by immigration officials in order to obtain an entry visa.

One of the people we met during my recent trip was Dr. Mitri Raheb, president of Dar al-Kalmia University College in Bethlehem, president of the Synod of the Evangelical Lutheran Church in Jordan and the Holy Land, and senior pastor of the Evangelical Lutheran Christmas Church in Bethlehem, Palestine. Dr. Raheb puts the way Herod "received" the Magi in context in his book titled *Faith in the Face of Empire: The Bible through Palestinian Eyes*:

In 2010 evangelical preacher Tony Campolo attended a theological conference in Bethlehem. Upon arrival at Ben Gurion Airport in Tel Aviv, Israeli officials told him that they would like to invite him for a cup of coffee in their offices and have a chat. For almost four hours he was questioned about his decision to attend a conference in Bethlehem, what he thought of the Kairos Palestine document, and how he knew some of these "radical" Palestinian theologians. This was supposed to be VIP treatment. . . . I told him, "So now you have experienced something biblical. Welcome to the Holy Land!"[3]

Perhaps the Magi were interrogated by Herod (and by his political and religious operatives) for the same reason international travelers are interrogated today: to control who enters and can move about territory ruled by an empire. Yet the visit of the Magi shows us that all people are drawn, yearn for, and seek liberation. Moreover, the Magi represent the idea that God's power to liberate humanity from sin and its oppression is not only praised and trusted by the Abrahamic people we read about in the Hebrew Testament. God's power to deliver humanity from oppression is also praised and trusted by people from other places, people who are not Hebrews, people whose identity is not defined by the tradition of Moses, Aaron, Samuel, David, Solomon, and the Hebrew judges and prophets.

The visit of the Magi is traditionally interpreted, understood, and proclaimed (preached, prayed, and sung) as meaning that God's determination to deliver (God's messianic power, purpose, passion, and presence) is praised and trusted by Gentiles, not Jews alone. Yet we should not limit our thinking at that point. Beyond the traditional interpretation, the visit of the Magi also reveals that God's messianic power, purpose, passion, and presence is always showing up—in subversive locations and ways and through unconventional people and processes—to confound and contradict human notions of empire.

No matter how much the Roman Empire thought it controlled, Caesar Augustus and Herod the Great (his puppet ruler in Palestine) did not control the will of God that brought about the birth of Jesus. Roman legionnaires could not prevent the sky from revealing the star the Magi saw. The Roman Empire could not prevent the Magi from being drawn to Jesus.

And the visit of the Magi calls us to stop expecting to find the purpose, power, passion, and presence for liberation in traditional power destinations. The Magi did not find Jesus in the ancient equivalent of Washington, DC, Paris, Moscow, London, New York City, Beijing, Riyadh, Tokyo, Mumbai, Tel Aviv, or any other location considered to be an imperial center of power.

The Magi were directed to find Jesus in Bethlehem, the city of David, located a few miles south of Jerusalem, the Palestinian capital city. The Magi found the purpose, power, passion, and presence of divine liberation on the outskirts of traditional power, not at the center of that power.

The Magi were not led to Rome, the capital of the Roman Empire. They did not make the pilgrimage to pay homage to Caesar Augustus in Rome, considered the center and highest example of human civilization. The Magi were led to Palestine, a land long occupied by foreign armies. The Magi were led to Palestine, whose indigenous people suffered from occupation-force policing backed by the Roman Empire. The Magi were led to seek the presence, purpose, power, and passion of divine liberation in an occupied land, and among an occupied people!

The Magi did not go to Jerusalem requesting an audience with Herod the Great, the puppet ruler of Palestine. The Magi went to Jerusalem asking, "Where is the child who has been born king of the Jews?"

The Magi understood that the human messenger of divine liberation was a young child, not a man. They were led to seek and find God's messenger of liberation in a child—a vulnerable person—not an adult showered in military, political, commercial, or social privilege.

The subversive truth of the visit of the Magi is that the liberating power, presence, purpose, and passion of God show up where worshippers of empire do not expect God. The liberating power, presence, purpose, and passion of God show up in ways worshippers of empire cannot predict, prevent, or prescribe. The liberating power, presence, purpose, and passion of God show up in people whom worshippers of empire overlook, disregard, and routinely oppress.

By now you should get the real point. The visit of the Magi to Jesus (the vulnerable child born under questionable circumstances and parented by a peasant mother and her working-class husband) in Bethlehem (a town located away from the center of power, wealth, and influence) is a divine affront to all claims of human empire.

Liberation from sin and every oppressive result sin produces is never associated with human empires. We who are followers of Jesus and tempted to advance the liberating purpose, power, presence, and passion of God through human empire should take heed of the words of Calgacus, a Briton chieftain who addressed fellow Britons concerning the Romans:

> Robbers of the world, having by their universal plunder exhausted the land, they rifle the deep. If the enemy be rich, they are rapacious; if he be poor, they lust for dominion; neither the east nor the west has been able to satisfy them. Alone among men they covet with equal eagerness poverty and riches. To robbery, slaughter, plunder, they give the lying name of empire; they make a desert and call it peace.[4]

History proves that these words ring true for every empire!

The visit of the Magi to pay homage to Jesus in Bethlehem shows not only that Jesus is the divine antidote to empire. Herod's response to the Magi also shows that empires always seek to enlist those who seek liberation, just as Herod tried to use the Magi as spies to locate Jesus. People who profess to be agents of the liberating power, presence, purpose, and passion of God revealed in Jesus should follow the example of the Magi. The Magi refused to spy for Herod. They did not return to Herod after they found Jesus, but "left for their own country by another road." *The Magi left without obtaining an exit visa.* The visit of the Magi, like everything about the gospel of Jesus, is subversive and contrary to the claims of the Roman, Spanish, French, German, British, American, Russian, Chinese, Israeli, and every other empire.

The visit of the Magi calls us to look to Jesus to find the highest and best answer to imperial claims and oppression, whether those claims are based on military, diplomatic, monetary, religious, cultural, national, ethnic, gender, or any other notion of power, privilege, and exceptionalism. The Magi, like the star they followed to Bethlehem, point us to Jesus. And Jesus points us to God!

■ In Jesus, we know that God is in the "empire-subverting business".

■ In Jesus, we know that God is in the "empire out-smarting business"!

■ In Jesus, we know that God is in the "empire-busting business"!

■ And in Jesus, the poor Palestinian child born in Bethlehem and praised there by the Magi, we know that God is in the "empire-outlasting business"!

The question for humanity is not whether God is somehow part of human empires. The issue is whether humans will recognize, praise, and trust God's liberating purpose, passion, power, and presence revealed in Jesus, the vulnerable and impoverished Palestinian boy of Bethlehem visited and worshipped by the Magi. And then the issue is whether we—like the Magi who refused to spy for Herod—will resist and reject the appeals of empires and emperors among us.

Let us, with the Magi, praise and trust God's liberating power, purpose, passion, and presence in Jesus. Let us, with the Magi, side with Jesus against Herod and all the other empires and emperors of this life. In seeking, praising, trusting, and following Jesus—and by renouncing and rejecting the appeals of empire—we become, with Jesus and the Magi who sought, found, and paid homage to Jesus, agents of God's liberating power, purpose, passion, and presence.

Discussion and Reflection Questions

1. In what ways are you and other followers of Jesus like the Magi about whom we read in the Gospel of Matthew?

2. What empires are you facing? What are those empires asking of and from you?

3. How are you and other followers of Jesus with whom you most closely associate following the example of the Magi, who refused to be complicit in King Herod's scheme to destroy Jesus?

4. What does the example of the Magi, who refused to obtain the equivalent of an exit visa before departing Judea, mean for you concerning undocumented immigrants?

Notes

1. Our group included a journalism professor from Northwestern University in Chicago, several faith leaders, scholars, and social justice activists associated with the Samuel DeWitt Proctor Conference, as well as two young adults involved in the Dream Defenders movement that arose in Florida after Trayvon Martin was shot to death by George Zimmerman.

2. One bearded young man from our group was questioned by Israeli immigration officials, at some length, about the meaning of his first and middle names (along with routine questions) before he was granted an entry visa.

3. Mitri Raheb, *Faith in the Face of Empire: The Bible through Palestinian Eyes* (Maryknoll, NY: Orbis Books), 2014, 56–57.

4. This quote is attributed to an indigenous chieftain who spoke to fellow Britons, and is found in *The Agricola and Germania* by Tacitus (the historian and son-in-law of Roman military commander and later politician Cnaeus Julius Agricola). See www.enotes.com/topics/agricola.

CHAPTER 8

Babel and Pentecost

So the LORD scattered them abroad from there over the face of all the earth, and they left off building the city. Therefore it was called Babel, because there the LORD confused the language of all the earth; and from there the LORD scattered them abroad over the face of all the earth. —Genesis 11:8-9

When the day of Pentecost had come, they were all together in one place. . . . All of them were filled with the Holy Spirit and began to speak in other languages, as the Spirit gave them ability. Now there were devout Jews from every nation under heaven living in Jerusalem. And at this sound the crowd gathered and was bewildered, because each one heard them speaking in the native language of each. —Acts 2:2,4-6

To many people, diversity and unity are conflicting ideas. In their minds, the way to have unity, strength, peace, and harmony is found in sameness. People who hold this view believe that peace, harmony, and prosperity are most likely to happen if people share the same beliefs about life, come from the same tribal or ethnic group, follow the same form of government, spend the same currency, and generally avoid involvements with people outside their group. Safety lies, according to this view, in sameness. Outsiders—meaning people who are different— are feared, distrusted, and run the risk of being branded as threats to peace. Diversity is cause for anxiety. The idolatrous notion that safety (salvation) is based on sameness is the foundation for xenophobia.

Genesis 11:1-9 proves that this concern is old, strong, and wrong. In this passage, people who shared the same language eventually feared being dispersed. So they decided to build a city and erect a tower in that city. The city and its tower would become the unifying force—they would be one people speaking one language in one place—that would guarantee their safety. Their reputation would be based on their sameness.

Some people interpret this passage as God's punishment of human ambition and ingenuity. They point to the city and its tower and the following words of God found in Genesis 11:6-7: "And the LORD said, 'Look, they are one people, and they have all one language; and this is only the beginning of what they will do; nothing that they propose to do will now be impossible for them. Come, let us go down, and confuse their language there, so that they will not understand one another's speech.'" According to that view, cultural diversity within humanity—our many languages, ethnicities, and identities—is God's way of punishing human arrogance and ingenuity for daring to build the first skyscraper.

That interpretation of Genesis 11:1-9 is not fair to God. Do we really think that the Creator of the universe is threatened by a municipal construction project? Are we dealing with a Being so insecure that a few people who put a city together and build a skyscraper get on his/her nerves? If God is that easily threatened, God should not be called good and gracious but petty and tyrannical.

Instead of reading the passage to mean that cultural diversity is divine punishment, we should understand it to show how cultural diversity is part of the great redemptive purpose of God. God is not threatened when people cooperate to construct cities and tall buildings. One-story buildings and rural settings are not entitled to divine favor.

What the passage shows is that God wants humans to be spread throughout the world and enjoy cultural diversity without being afraid. If there is a condemnation in the passage—and I use the word *if* intentionally—it condemns the idea that sameness is the way to salvation. We are one people because we have a common Creator, not because we speak the same language or live in the same location. Our oneness lies in who we are before God, not who we are physically related to by human ancestry and geography. God loves our diversity. God intentionally caused our diversity. God is glorified by our diversity.

The Babel passage also highlights our human tendency to resist obeying God. Instead of being fruitful and spreading throughout the world, the inhabitants of Babel insisted on being a local tribe. For them, salvation meant tribal identity and location. God's response was to mix them up linguistically. The New Revised Standard Version of the Bible unfortunately uses the word *confuse* regarding language. A better rendering of the text would interpret the passage as God deciding to "mix" their language. The people scattered after their language became mixed. Cultural diversity—mixing the languages—was God's way of getting the people to move from one location and disperse throughout the world. God was at work at Babel.

And as humans migrated, the challenge became whether we would retain a sense of our kinship under one Creator. Would distance and diversity cause us to deny our common humanity? Would we glorify God in many languages and places, or would we decide that only our place and our language truly deserve divine favor? *Would we try to re-create Babel?* If so, what does God do?

The rest of the Bible answers that question. Although humans come from one Creator and share common ancestry, we have stubbornly held on to the ancient fear of diversity. We view people who are different as dangerous, whether they are different because they speak a different language, worship in different ways, come from different places, or are different in other ways.

■ People who are lesbian, gay, bisexual, and/or transgender are considered dangerous because their sexual orientation and gender identity are different.

■ Muslims are considered dangerous because their religion and traditions are different.

■ People are dangerous if they belong to a different political party.

■ The nation of Israel views Palestinians as dangerous because they are different.

Fear of people who are different lies at the root of much hate, oppression, and injustice in human history. Although God loves diversity, history proves that even religious people do not love and trust God enough to love the diversity that God created. In fact, we have often used religion to justify prejudice, bigotry, and injustice as shown by our petty denominational rivalries and bigotry. This is also seen in the hateful and fear-based demands by certain US politicians and white Christian nationalists to put up a wall to keep Mexicans out. And it is shown by the demands by certain US politicians and nationalists that Muslim immigrants be banned or screened more closely than other immigrants.

This leads us to Acts 2:1-21 and the vivid description of community in diversity at Pentecost. Just as diversity of languages and cultures is seen in Genesis to be the work of God, the sense that community is possible in the midst of diversity is shown at Pentecost to be the work of God. In Babel and Pentecost, God is working. But while God is working in Babel to scatter humanity, at Pentecost we see scattered humanity coming to hear the gospel of divine grace and truth in one place, yet each hearing that gospel in the language of their heritage.

At Pentecost the Holy Spirit moves on a handful of followers of Jesus, who become messengers of God's Good News. Just as God worked at Babel to mix languages so that people began to scatter, God moved at Pentecost to mix the languages spoken by the first followers of Jesus so that scattered people would learn what God has done in Jesus Christ to make us one people.

At Pentecost the Spirit of God shows that we are not one people because we speak the same language. We are not one people because we live in the same country. We are not one people because we worship the same way. We are one people of many languages, many places, and many ways of worship because God has made us and loves us, as demonstrated in the life, death, and resurrection of Jesus Christ.

God created us for glorious living in our diversity. God created us to live in peace and fellowship with one another in our diversity. God blessed us to be different because diversity is divinely favored. In doing so, God declares that cultural differences do not make us dangerous to one another or to God. Rather than fearing and mistreating one another based on cultural differences, we are to affirm one another as children of God who speak different languages, live in different places, and are different because God loves diversity.

Our sinful ignorance and bigotry cause us to fear diversity, view it as threatening, and mistreat people who are different. It is one thing to admit that we act this way because we are afraid to trust God's gift of diversity. It is something else when we claim that cultural diversity is divine punishment. We do a tremendous disservice to the grace and goodness of God when we try to justify our prejudice and bigotry towards people who are different.

Babel and Pentecost also show that God is always nudging us out of our comfort zones. The Holy Spirit's gift of languages was as much of a surprise at Pentecost as the mixed languages were at Babel. God pushes us, nudges us, and drives us from our comfort zones, away from familiar notions of oneness by sameness, and out of our insular views of life and relationships. In Jesus Christ, we witness God's love to different people, including people who are oppressed because they are different. And in the Holy Spirit, we see God's love and the gospel of love being spread to all people, whatever their language, ancestry, or homeland.

Babel and Pentecost remind us that children of God speak in many languages. Children of God come in different colors, sexual orientations, and gender identities. Children of God worship in many different ways. When we grow to understand God's glorious purpose in diversity, then we will celebrate what the Holy Spirit does to nudge us out of our comfort zones.

Consider the ways that we repeat the Babel experience. Building walls around ourselves reminds us of Babel. The Great Wall of China, the Berlin Wall, the Israeli-Gaza Wall, and a wall along the US border with Mexico show how much we need the Holy Spirit to nudge us. Anti-immigration laws show how much we need the Holy Spirit to nudge us. Denominationalism and the mindset by which we build cities, towers, and walls to keep people who are different out of our churches, out of our schools, out of our communities, and out of our lives remind us that we need to be nudged by the Holy Spirit. In a sense, the push to divert money for public education into charter schools resembles the effort to repeat the Babel experience.

The good news, from Babel and Pentecost, is that God nudges! Hallelujah! God nudges us out of our fears. God nudges us to new understandings about fellowship, peace, prosperity, and community. Babel says that we must expect to be divinely nudged, disturbed, and even frustrated. Pentecost reminds us that God nudges us so that we can grow into deeper and wider notions of community.

So we sing "we are one in the Spirit" because the Spirit nudges us. We love in the Spirit. We live in the Spirit. We embrace people who are different in the Spirit. We are nudged as the Holy Spirit impels us toward becoming one people of many languages, tribes, and nationalities who live for God.

Discussion and Reflection Questions

1. How do your neighborhood, faith community, and circle of personal relationships resemble Babel? How do they resemble Pentecost?

2. In what ways has the Holy Spirit nudged you away from the false notion of salvation through sameness (Babel) and toward being "Pentecostal" in the sense of embracing, celebrating, and affirming diversity? How did you respond? What was the reaction from others when you did so?

3. What lessons do you take about immigration from the disruptive migration from Babel and the assembly of diverse persons in Jerusalem at Pentecost?

4. When have you heard other sermons, teaching, or discussion about Babel and Pentecost that mentioned human diversity, migration, and treatment of immigrants? How have those teachings affected your perspectives on diversity and the treatment of immigrants and strangers?

CHAPTER 9

Lessons of Love and Justice from a Vineyard

As soon as Jezebel heard that Naboth had been stoned and was dead, Jezebel said to Ahab, "Go, take possession of the vineyard of Naboth the Jezreelite, which he refused to give you for money; for Naboth is not alive, but dead." As soon as Ahab heard that Naboth was dead, Ahab set out to go down to the vineyard of Naboth the Jezreelite, to take possession of it. Then the word of the LORD came to Elijah the Tishbite, saying: Go down to meet King Ahab of Israel, who rules in Samaria; he is now in the vineyard of Naboth, where he has gone to take possession. You shall say to him, "Thus says the LORD: Have you killed, and also taken possession?" —1 Kings 21:15-19

One of the constant issues of life is to realize the theological, moral, ethical, social, and personal meanings of our interactions and relationships. Words such as *love* and *justice* speak to our interconnectedness. As the poet John Donne famously wrote, "No man [person] is an island."

But the sin that drives us to believe that we are unaccountable to God also inspires the idea that we can treat others as we please. We somehow believe that if we are powerful enough, cunning enough, or ruthless enough we can have our way.

A commoner named Naboth once lived in Jezreel, one of the most fertile regions in Palestine. He had a vineyard beside the royal palace of Ahab of Samaria, ruler of the northern kingdom of Israel. King Ahab wanted Naboth's vineyard so he could convert it into a vegetable garden. But this was ancestral property. Naboth refused all offers to trade or sell the vineyard property because it was part of his heritage. Ahab became so depressed by Naboth's rejection that he took to his bed.

But Queen Jezebel, Ahab's wife, was not so easily spurned. Acting in the name and authority of the king, Jezebel sent letters ordering that a public meeting be held. The letters ordered that Naboth was to be publicly and falsely accused of slandering God and the king at that meeting, and then executed by stoning. Her instructions were followed. Naboth was falsely accused, wrongfully convicted, and publicly executed. Jezebel then told her husband, King Ahab, to claim possession of the vineyard. But when Ahab did so, he was confronted by a prophet of God named Elijah. Elijah did not welcome Ahab but denounced Ahab's ownership claim and possession of Naboth's vineyard. Elijah pronounced doom on Ahab's personal and political future.

Ahab and Jezebel show us how power can be misused to manipulate people and events to achieve unjust (meaning unloving) results. Naboth reminds us that vulnerable people can be mistreated and victimized even when they are acting within their rights. Elijah demonstrates how prophetic people should respond to injustice—and that injustice must not be ignored but rather denounced as a crime against God and our neighbors.

Yes, self-centeredness will cause people to pout when they can't have their way. The covetousness of Ahab is no different from the covetousness of people everywhere. Look anywhere and you'll find people like Naboth who are threatened by the covetousness of others for their land, water, or other possessions.

■ Palestinians whose homes and lands are being seized and who are being thrown off their land by some Israelis, with the support from the Israeli government and military, are like Naboth. Some of the suffering of those Palestinians, including poverty and sickness, is caused by the same injustice that Naboth experienced from Queen Jezebel and King Ahab. During the 2016 presidential campaign, neither Donald Trump nor Hillary Clinton said anything about that decades-long violation of moral and international law. Bernie Sanders was the only leading presidential candidate to mention it.[1]

■ Gentrification of urban neighborhoods and similar displacement efforts by land speculators and commercial developers that result in people being forced from their land by "urban renewal," zoning changes, and similar dispossession schemes are like what happened to Naboth.

■ Whenever people of limited means are threatened by wealthy interests, they are like Naboth. They are content with and trying to enjoy what they have. But their contentment and joy is threatened by the greed of people who have more power, be it financial, official, physical, or some combination of the three.

Yes, self-centeredness causes people to plot against others in order to get their way (as Jezebel plotted against Naboth). Yes, people will intentionally cooperate with and participate in wicked schemes against others to obtain favor with others in power. Yes, those plots and schemes result in real injuries to people. Yes, positions are sometimes gained by wrongful might.

Queen Jezebel's scheme to get Naboth's vineyard worked only because others intentionally cooperated with and participated in it. It worked because people in official positions agreed to plot against Naboth. People in official positions agreed to fabricate false accusations against him. Other people agreed to make those false accusations. Then others agreed to find Naboth guilty of something he never did and then to kill him in the name of justice. Naboth suffered the loss of his life and his vineyard when greed became powerful enough to produce injustice.

Much of the suffering endured by Native Americans today can be traced to the sort of injustice that Naboth experienced after Queen Jezebel acted to take his vineyard and give it to King Ahab.

■ In an essay titled "Racism and American Law" in the book *Law Against the People: Essays to Demystify Law, Order, and the Courts,* Haywood Burns wrote how 119 California Native American tribes gave up more than half the state of California in exchange for perpetual ownership of 7.5 million acres.

■ Due to pressure from white politicians, the US Senate never ratified the treaties under which the Native Americans gave up their land in exchange for the 7.5 million acres.

■ The Indian Bureau had negotiated the treaties in 1851 but never told the tribes about the failure to ratify.

■ In 1905 the 7.5 million acres that Native Americans thought were theirs were sold to white settlers and land speculators.[2]

This story about Naboth and his vineyard, Ahab, Jezebel, and Elijah is relevant for today. Self-centered people with enough power can manipulate law and government officials to accomplish results that have nothing to do with justice and everything to do with their lust for what belongs to others. That is how voting in a presidential election was shut down in Florida and how five justices of the US Supreme Court later arranged to decide the outcome of the 2000 presidential election. And it sheds light on how people who claim to be evangelical followers of Jesus turned a blind eye to the misogyny, military adventurism, racism, sexism, xenophobia, and crass materialism of Donald Trump and voted to elect him president of the United States.

Naboth could have been saved if the people who received the letters Jezebel sent under Ahab's seal had been more interested in love and justice. But they weren't. They loved being popular and powerful more than they loved Naboth. They loved the idea of doing a favor for the king more than they loved doing right by a commoner. Similarly, white self-professed evangelical followers of Jesus who consider themselves "good Christians" overwhelmingly voted for Donald Trump because they preferred access to power over liberty and equality for persons they consider "others" (racial minorities, Muslims, immigrants, women and girls who dare to live free from patriarchy and who reject the heresy of male supremacy, and people who are lesbian, gay, bisexual, and transgender).

Naboth was executed for a crime he did not commit. Yes, people are often disenfranchised, defrauded, and even killed for official reasons based on fabricated facts.

■ No weapons of mass destruction have been found in Iraq. Every life lost or scarred by that fabricated war is a Naboth! And any politician who supported the decision to invade Iraq behaved like Queen Jezebel. In the US House of Representatives, Congresswoman Barbara Lee of California cast the only vote against the authorization for the use of military force (AUMF) after the September 11, 2001 terrorist attacks.[3]

■ No charges have been brought against some of the people now being held by the United States in Guantanamo. Each uncharged or falsely charged person held there is a Naboth! Prophetic followers of Jesus should have followed the example of Elijah and confronted President George W. Bush, President Barack Obama, their national security staffs, and the other political leaders who are responsible for the continued Naboth-like treatment of Guantanamo detainees.

■ The United States leads the industrialized world in mass incarceration. Much of the rise in our prison population since 1980 can be traced to the willingness of people from all walks of life and every political and religious persuasion to treat substance abuse as a crime rather than an illness. Every person who has a felony conviction for possession of illegal drugs is a Naboth! Unfortunately, prophetic followers of Jesus have not behaved as Elijah did. Prophetic followers of Jesus did not condemn the policies put in place by President Bill Clinton that produced drastic incarceration increases.[4]

■ Many people lost their homes through foreclosure in the financial meltdown of the past decade. Information has come to light that some banks and other lenders have used unscrupulous practices, altered documents, and even misrepresented facts in order to put borrowers into foreclosure.[5] Those borrowers are modern versions of Naboth! Again, the injustices committed against those former homeowners should have been challenged with Elijah-like courage and integrity by prophetic followers of Jesus.

Despite the self-centered and wicked spirit and schemes of powerful people like Ahab and Jezebel, God always has people around who love truth and justice enough to denounce oppression and injustice. God has some Elijah-like people around who do the prophetic work of confronting and denouncing greed, dishonesty, and oppression. The Spirit of God that inspired Elijah to confront Ahab is still moving. Let me suggest some ways that you and I can be part of God's Elijah-like response to the Ahab-Jezebel mindset and movement of our time and place.

Keep your heart and mind filled with the love and justice of God. Injustice and oppression always operate as violations of divine love and justice. Whenever people violate the divine rule of love and justice by self-centeredness and greed, they are susceptible to mistreating their neighbors. The way to be an Elijah-like prophetic force in the world begins and ends with focusing our hearts and minds on God's love and justice. Anything that violates God's love and justice is a threat to our neighbors—the people who are like Naboth.

Denounce greed, violence, and other oppressive attitudes and conduct. Jezebel's scheme to kill Naboth and steal his vineyard could have been blocked if the officials who received the letters she wrote in Ahab's name had refused to go along with the program. See the injustice around us. Don't hide from it or ignore it. Look at it. Denounce and oppose it. Confront and expose the people associated with it.

Speak up for oppressed and vulnerable people. Too often we heed the message to "let it go" when injustice happens. We look the other way. We refuse to get involved. We don't want to make waves. We want to get along with powerful people even though we know they're doing wicked things and oppressing our vulnerable brothers and sisters.

But God sent Elijah to make waves and speak up even for the rights of a dead man. In 1 Kings 21:17-19 we read: "Then the word of the LORD came to Elijah the Tishbite, saying: Go down to meet King Ahab of Israel, who rules in Samaria; he is now in the vineyard of Naboth, where he has gone to take possession. You shall say to him, 'Thus says the LORD: Have you killed, and also taken possession?'" Ahab and Jezebel thought that

Naboth's claim was extinguished, but Elijah was sent by God to press that claim despite the death of its owner. The Holy Spirit authorizes us to act in the same way on behalf of oppressed people.

Declare God's judgment against people who practice injustice and oppression. Unjust people are guilty of two crimes. In the first place, they don't love God. Secondly, they don't love their neighbors. When we won't confront them, denounce their oppressive conduct, and declare God's judgment against it, these people become comfortable and content with their unjustly obtained possessions and relationships. They believe their future is secure when in fact they've been doomed.

People who, like Elijah, are inspired with a sense of God's love and justice know that people who practice injustice and oppression need to be confronted and warned. Perhaps they will see their wrongfulness and seek forgiveness. Perhaps they will be moved to correct the harm they've done, heal the wounds they've inflicted, and make restitution for what has been unjustly gained. But it takes people whose lives are transformed by the same Spirit that moved Elijah to declare God's judgment to them.

The Holy Spirit will send us to declare God's judgment to people who are comfortable with the fruit of injustice. God will be glorified as you and I deliver the message that injustice may appear to be profitable, but it always results in disaster.[6]

The message Elijah delivered to Ahab is as true for our time as it was for Ahab: "Because you have sold yourself to do what is evil in the sight of the LORD, I will bring disaster on you; I will consume you" (1 Kings 21:20-21). The Ahab people of our time and place need some Elijah people to deliver that message. They need to hear it so that they can be convicted of their crimes against God and their neighbors. They need to hear it so that they can seek God's forgiveness and trust God's grace. They need to hear it so that they can make restitution and reparation for the injustice they have committed. They need to hear it so that God's law of love and justice will be vindicated among us.

The Spirit of God is with us to be Elijah people in an Ahab and Jezebel world and time. The Spirit of God that lived most fully in Jesus is with us. The Spirit of God that does not wink at injustice and oppression is with us. The Spirit of God that witnesses every wrongful deed, knows every wicked scheme, and is wounded along with every person who suffers from these deeds and schemes is with us. The Spirit of God sends us to confront, denounce, and declare God's judgment on injustice and oppression by Ahab and Jezebel bullies against vulnerable people like Naboth.

Let it be said that the Spirit of God moved us to stand up for Naboth people and their right to be treated with dignity, love, and fairness. Let the Spirit that moved Elijah, and that moved even more powerfully and effectively in Jesus, cause us to show up where we aren't expected and even when we aren't welcomed.

Follow that Spirit and speak up for Naboth children oppressed by unjust people who deny their right to a decent education. Follow that Spirit and speak up for Naboth people living in communities threatened by Ahab and Jezebel forces who would pollute and steal their air, land, and water. Follow that Spirit and speak up for Naboth people oppressed by greedy people and companies who cheat people out of the healthcare they need and deserve. Follow that Spirit and speak out against anti-immigrant rhetoric and policies. Follow that Spirit and speak out against laws that discriminate against people who are lesbian, gay, bisexual, and transgender. Follow that Spirit that inspired Elijah and Jesus.

Follow that Spirit so that the Ahab people of our time and place will know that they are not God. Follow that Spirit in obedience to the life of Jesus. Follow the Spirit that moved Elijah to confront and declare God's judgment against Ahab and that moved Jesus to confront and change the world.

Follow that Spirit! Live in the power of that Spirit. Love in the strength of that Spirit. Trust that Spirit. Be strong and courageous by that Spirit. Be God's prophetic people in obedience to that Spirit. Live to the glory of God in the power of that Spirit!

Discussion and Reflection Questions

1. How have Ahab and Naboth situations occurred where you live? What was your response to them? How did other followers of Jesus respond?

2. How did you and other followers of Jesus support people like Naboth who were threatened by people who behaved like Ahab and Jezebel?

3. How does the issue of Palestinian sovereignty resemble the lesson of Ahab, Jezebel, Naboth, and Elijah? How does the issue of Native American land ownership (as expressed at Standing Rock in 2016) resemble this lesson?

4. What have you, your faith leaders and religious educators, and your faith community done that resembles the actions of Elijah concerning displacement of people from their neighborhoods, ancestral lands, and other places?

Notes

1. See http://www.huffingtonpost.com/entry/bernie-sanders-hillary-clinton-israel_us_57114f60e4b0060ccda353ab, accessed January 9, 2017.

2. See Haywood Burns, "Racism and American Law," in *Law Against the People: Essays to Demystify Law, Order, and the Courts* Robert Lefcourt ed., (Vintage Books, A Division of Random House, 1971), 38, 39–41. The Treaty with the Si-Yan-Te, etc. of 1851 involved the California land fraud on the 119 California tribes.

3. See https://lee.house.gov/about/biography accessed January 9, 2017.

4. See https://www.theguardian.com/us-news/2015/apr/28/bill-clinton-calls-for-end-mass-incarceration accessed January 9, 2017.

5. See https://newrepublic.com/article/117912/reparations-how-mortgage-market-hurts-african-americans accessed January 9, 2017.

6. The official and private injustices inflicted on Native Americans have left stains on US history that cannot be denied or erased. The same is true for the injustices of American slavery, sexism, and capitalism. The stolen presidential election of 2000 produced a presidency that will be forever marked by the national security disaster of the September 11, 2001, terrorist attacks, the foreign policy disaster of the fabricated war in Iraq, the mishandled war in Afghanistan, and the economic meltdown in the fall of 2008.

CHAPTER 10

Finding Love Songs in Our Faith Book[1]

The voice of my beloved! Look, he comes, leaping upon the mountains, bounding over the hills. My beloved is like a gazelle or a young stag. Look, there he stands behind our wall, gazing in at the windows, looking through the lattice. My beloved speaks and says to me: "Arise, my love, my fair one, and come away; for now the winter is past, the rain is over and gone. The flowers appear on the earth; the time of singing has come, and the voice of the turtledove is heard in our land. The fig tree puts forth its figs, and the vines are in blossom; they give forth fragrance. Arise, my love, my fair one, and come away. —Song of Songs 2:8-13

As I was thinking about this passage, one of the memorable lines from the movie *A League of Their Own* kept running through my mind. That movie is about a fictional 1922 women's baseball team managed by a salty-mouthed former big-league manager named Jimmy Dugan, played by Tom Hanks. Those of you who have seen the movie will recall Jimmy Dugan taking one of the women players to task in front of the whole team about a defensive mistake she made that caused their team to lose a two-run lead. When she began crying, Dugan shouted at her, "Are you crying? There's no crying in baseball!"

The Song of Songs, along with Job, Psalms, Proverbs, and Ecclesiastes, is part of the section of the Bible known as Wisdom literature. This book, however, is unlike Job, which is a deep look into the struggle to reconcile faith in the goodness of God when terrible things happen to good people. It isn't about prayer, praise, and worship like Psalms. The Song of Songs isn't about wisdom in the same way that we read in Proverbs. And it isn't about any of the topics in Ecclesiastes.

The Song of Songs, in fact, doesn't mention God, faith, covenant, salvation, forgiveness, repentance, or any of the other great subjects we encounter in the rest of the Hebrew Bible and New Testament. The book is, quite plainly, a series of poems between two lovers. They describe one another in terms that are vivid, romantic, and erotic.

In the Song of Songs we find love poems in our faith book. We read expressions of heartfelt desire, longing, and admiration by two people. We get no hints that these poems are about procreation. We read a woman speaking about love, passion, and sensuality on equal terms with her male lover, and without the filter of patriarchy. We read about human sexuality without religious ceremonies, preachers, priests, and beliefs about marriage.

And like Jimmy Dugan was shocked to find crying in his historically male-dominated sport, we are surprised to find this in our faith book. Why is it there? What does it mean? How are we to make sense of it?

One way is to ignore these love poems altogether. We rarely hear sermons based on the Song of Songs. When was the last time you heard of a Bible study group delving into the Song of Songs the way we study other books in the Bible? Even adult classes probably avoid reading and discussing the Song of Songs in Sunday school. Have you delved into the Song of Songs in a personal Bible study? Probably not. It's as if this book isn't part of the sacred text.

The title of this book is Song of Songs. That's a Hebrew way of saying it's the best of the Songs (think of "King of kings," "Lord of lords," and Holy of holies"). Now ponder the irony that religious people, professional people who affirm that the Bible is authoritative, individually and collectively avoid reading, hearing, studying, discussing, pondering, preaching, and being influenced by a work of Scripture titled "Song of Songs." Ponder why religious people have hidden from this portion of the Wisdom books in Scripture.

Another way to understand the Song of Songs is to simply accept these love poems for what they plainly are—honest, romantic, erotic, and sensual. They express the heartfelt yearning of two people who love each other. These are love poems by people who openly announce how much they miss one another, how they long to be together, and how they view each other as physically attractive and sexually desirable. They constitute wisdom by reminding us that sexual attraction, sexuality, romance, sensuality, and erotic desire are integral to our humanity and should be embraced by people of faith.

But instead of accepting these love poems for what they plainly are—healthy, honest, and sensual expressions of romantic desire by two lovers—religious people have done something else. We've tried to sanitize them by calling them allegorical. So in Judaism the Songs are considered symbolic of the way God woos Israel. Christian theologians view the Songs as symbolic of the relationship between Christ and his Bride (the church).

Like Jimmy Dugan, religious folks are too often unwilling to accept and affirm that romance, sexual attraction, and eroticism have a place in the life of faithful people. We're so uncomfortable dealing honestly with the subject of sensuality, sexuality, and romantic love that we've converted these beautiful poems about romance and sexual desire between two human lovers into a theological framework about the relationship between God and humanity—as if God and humanity are engaged in lovers' talk—despite the obvious fact that God, salvation, covenant, and none of the other salvation issues in the Hebrew Bible and New Testament are mentioned.

That, my friends, is what can be charitably called "ducking a sensitive subject." We might also say that it exposes how religious people have infected and polluted faith in God's goodness with prudish anxieties and phobia concerning sex, sexuality, and romantic desire.

Perhaps one reason religious people have dodged the subject of romance, sexual desire, and sexuality that runs through the Song of Songs is because what we read in the Songs doesn't fit our notion of morality. The lovers in the Songs aren't married. That forces us to face the reality that erotic desire isn't limited to marriage. We must deal with the truth that romance and sexual attraction are real, powerful, and desirable without wedding bells, marriage vows, and religious views about marriage. That makes more than a few people uncomfortable!

And it especially doesn't make some people comfortable to read such open talk about sensual desire from a woman's perspective. The Song of Songs is one of the few books in the Bible where a woman's voice and perspective is prominent (which has led some scholars to speculate that this collection might have been compiled by a woman).

This is no shy, coy woman. She is what the late United Methodist minister and author Linda Hollies termed "a bodacious woman." She speaks of the voice of her beloved, how he looks, how he stands, and how he gazes in at her "at the windows, looking through the lattice" (Song of Songs 2:9). She declares with unrestrained delight how her lover courts her with the words in Song of Songs 2:10-13:

> My beloved speaks and says to me: "Arise, my love, my fair one, and come away; for now the winter is past, the rain is over and gone. The flowers appear on the earth; the time of singing has come, and the voice of the turtledove is heard in our land. The fig tree puts up its figs, and the vines are in blossom; they give forth fragrance. Arise, my love, my fair one, and come away." (ESV)

This is a call to a lover's rendezvous. This is, to be sure, not the stuff for children's church or a Disney family movie. But it is honest and rustic talk that lovers share. It isn't illicit, immoral, or illegal. It isn't perverted or obscene. It isn't pornographic or exploitative. It is merely how a person in love expresses her desire to be with her lover.

In the Song of Songs, faithful people are invited to affirm the reality that romance, physical attraction, sexuality, and sensuality are part of the blessings of being human. We're invited to look at physical attraction as a joy to accept, not a burden to feel guilty about. We're invited to see spontaneity and declarations of sensual desire and erotic delight apart from procreation, apart from marriage, and apart from anything other than being human. And because this collection of love poems is part of the Wisdom literature in the Bible, we're invited to understand and celebrate that sexuality, sensuality, and eroticism are integral aspects of human character to be celebrated, not shamed.

But we haven't done that. Instead of affirming sexuality, sensuality, and eroticism and helping people understand how they function within the life of faith, rabbis and preachers across the ages have dodged the erotic realities of our humanity and sexuality. Instead of encouraging faithful people to read and celebrate the Songs for what they plainly are—romantic and sensual love poems—we too often act as if romance, sensuality, and eroticism have nothing to do with religious faith.

The Song of Songs tells us that faithful people are not merely Bible readers and praise makers. Faithful peoples do more than pray, preach, and engage in acts of compassion and deliverance. Faithful people are also passionate lovers! Faithful people live in the joy and beauty of their sexuality and sensuality. Faithful people are attracted to other people and express that attraction in vivid words that can sometimes be erotic. That's part of the "good" that God declares for us in Genesis.

There are love songs in our faith book because God has gifted humans with the capacity to be lovers. God has gifted us with the capacity to be attracted to one another, physically, sexually, and without shame. The moral aspect of that reality involves being honest and fair in the way we exercise those gifts.

The first part of that honesty and fairness involves accepting and affirming sexuality, sensuality, erotic desire, and romance as gifts from God. This is something faithful people must accept for ourselves and respect in others. Sexuality, sensuality, erotic desire, and romance are not wicked. They aren't bad. They aren't hostile to God's will. And they aren't to be treated as any or all of those things by religion. Scripture doesn't teach that. The fact that the Song of Songs has been preserved across centuries and included in the Bible shows the exact opposite to be true.

The reality that sexuality, sensuality, erotic desire, and the romance that goes with it are gifts from God is also something we must help children understand as they enter and begin to confront the sensual and sexual newness of puberty. Instead of refusing to talk with youth about sexuality, sensuality, erotic desire, and romance or—even worse—denouncing those subjects as off-limits or somehow evil, the Song of Songs shows that understanding and accepting these features of our humanity are required to be morally and emotionally whole and healthy.

Another part of that honesty and fairness revealed by the Song of Songs is that sexuality, sensuality, erotic desire, and romance are from God for mutual enjoyment, not exploitation, oppression, or manipulation. The Song of Songs certainly includes illustrations that are sensual, even erotic. But nowhere do we get the impression that the lovers are exploiting, abusing, or somehow oppressing one another.

Nothing suggests that these people are viewing each other merely as sex objects to be casually used and discarded like disposable products. And to put it bluntly, the Song of Songs does not somehow validate Donald Trump's claim of several years ago that his maleness, celebrity, and wealth gave him a license to grope the genitalia of women and march unannounced and without permission into areas where women were in states of undress.[2]

Throughout the Songs the passages show that each lover is devoted to the other. Each lover is focused on being with and pleasing the other. Each lover is interested in the well-being of the other. Yes, we read sensual and erotic language. But this is not pornography; none of the passages are offered to arouse or titillate the reader. These poems are honest expressions of heartfelt yearning and desire by people who love and are devoted to each other.

The fact that we find all of this in our faith book should encourage people of religious faith and the faith communities to which we belong to be open and affirming about the blessings of sex, sexuality, romance, and passion—about the blessings that people who are committed to each other can share because God has created us as we are. We are God's people. Sexuality and sensuality are not gifts to us from God to make the life of faith burdensome, but to make life and faith joyful, delightful, and vibrant.

Like many other pastors I know and countless more I don't know, I've learned to be available, responsive, and alert to calls for help in unexpected times and circumstances. But nothing in my ministry formation prepared me to respond to the reality of human sexuality, congregational unity, pastoral care, and the various challenges and opportunities to experience and enlarge what we mean by "covenant" when it comes to human sexuality. Human sexuality is as real as anything else one encounters in pastoral ministry, but I wasn't educated about it in church, college, or seminary.

My parents talked with me about sex. But I don't recall any conversations with my parents or youth leaders about human sexuality during my youth. I don't recall any church conferences about human sexuality. I don't think my experience is very different from other congregational leaders.

If my experience is typical, then it's probably safe to say that many— if not a majority—of the people who lead congregations reached adulthood like I did: with a very limited understanding about human sexuality. Perhaps we had conversations with our parents or other elders about sex and sensuality. Youth leaders occasionally and delicately talked about the topic of sex and dating. But I have yet to meet any pastoral peer who grew up in a family or congregation where human sexuality was mentioned.

It's not unfair or inaccurate to say that when it comes to the issue of human sexuality, religious people in the United States have avoided serious thinking, honest conversation, and open-minded dialogue. I trace our aversion to engage the issue of sexuality by serious thought, honest discourse, and open-minded conversation to one thing: we have a phobia about human sexuality. We're afraid to admit that we're afraid about sexuality. We're uncomfortable thinking about it. We're uneasy. As individuals, families, congregations, communities, clergypersons, and members of a society where free expression of opinions is supposedly valued, we've been afraid to think, speak, and work to lovingly understand sexuality, one of the basic aspects of our humanity.

Sexuality has historically been left off the list of subjects we recruit educators to teach in high school. Sexuality has traditionally not been included among the issues seminary faculty and students analyze. In the minority of seminaries that include courses on human sexuality in the curricula, the courses aren't required. So no one should be surprised that our congregations aren't comfortable dealing with sexuality.

I haven't been immune or exempt from the fearful aversion to addressing sexuality. But I'm convinced that the aversion has done great harm to individuals, families, faith communities, and our desire to be agents of God's love and truth in the world. I've seen firsthand the pain and fear of families faced with the prospect that some aspect of a loved one's sexuality will become known. I've witnessed the anxiety of parents, grandparents, siblings, and other relatives.

And I've witnessed firsthand the way fear and misunderstanding can work cruel results. I have known and hurt for people who were afraid to come to worship because they expected to be shunned or blamed because of their sexuality. I've tried to protect and comfort family members who were afraid to ask their congregation to pray for a loved one who was diagnosed with AIDS. I've known the special anxiety young people feel when they are afraid to talk with parents, other relatives, and church leaders about sexuality. I've seen and heard pastors and other clergy demonize vulnerable children, teenagers, and adults simply because those people are different because of their sexuality. And I've seen preachers and other church people mount and support political efforts that portray people who are gay, lesbian, bisexual, or transgender as threats to family cohesion and societal order based solely on their sexuality.

In 2004 I observed pastors rally and collect signatures for an amendment to the Arkansas constitution that banned same-sex marriage. In 2008 many pastors and other people of faith mounted another petition drive for an initiated act banning unmarried cohabiting persons from becoming adoptive or foster parents. Both efforts were on the ballot during presidential election years. Both measures were adopted by Arkansas voters by wide margins. In 2010 the act initiated in 2008 that banned unmarried cohabiting persons from becoming adoptive or foster parents was declared unconstitutional by the Arkansas Supreme Court as a violation of the right of privacy guaranteed by our state constitution.

So when New Millennium Church was organized in 2009, I prayed that we would be different. I prayed that we would be people who are not bound by a fear of difference but who are inspired by God's love to be "inclusive, welcoming, and progressive followers of Jesus Christ." But how would we live out the challenges surrounding the issue of sexuality? I will share what we've done and how it has affected us.

We affirm oneness and welcome all persons in God's love during every Sunday worship service. Our congregation recites the following "Affirmation of Oneness and Purpose" each Sunday morning: "We praise and worship God, together. We petition God, together. We proclaim God, together. We welcome all persons in God's love, together. We live for God, in every breath and heartbeat, by the power of the Holy Spirit, as followers of Jesus Christ, together." This affirmation is made immediately following what we call the "Greet and Fellowship Moment," in which everyone is invited to greet and be welcomed by everyone else as we "welcome all persons in God's love together."

Why is this important? Almost every person in our congregation has lived through times of legalized segregation and religiously inspired discrimination against people who are different because of race, gender, and sexuality. But we have come to know God's love as expressed and demonstrated in Jesus Christ. In Christ, we have come to understand God's love for and acceptance of all persons. In Christ, we have come to realize that humanity involves a wonderful and God-ordained diversity. In Christ, we have experienced the meaning of being one with God and others by the unifying work of grace and the Holy Spirit. Somehow, our congregation was inspired to affirm our commitment to oneness and to "welcome all persons in God's love" because we sincerely trust that this is what it means to be one with God in Christ.

Pastors have a prophetic duty to proclaim God's love in ways that welcome all people. Congregational life isn't defined by the personality of a pastor, but pastors have profound potential on that life by the way we proclaim the gospel of Jesus Christ. I'm struck, however, by how often pastors seem unwilling or unable to grasp and present God's love for all persons, especially concerning sexuality, consensual human relationships, and the realities that define human diversity.

I'm no model preacher by any means. But I was led to preach about the encounter Jesus had with a Samaritan woman at Jacob's Well for the inaugural worship service of New Millennium Church on May 31, 2009. I tried to present what that encounter meant to her and means for us in a sermon titled "Give Me This Water!"

By his deliberate encounter with the Samaritan woman, Jesus revealed to her and to us that we can never be truly refreshed and rejuvenated by a well-and-bucket approach to life and faith. We need "living water" that is invigorating, soothing, and cooling as we experience the challenges, conflicts, defeats, insults, and tragedies of our journeys. We need a source of strength and vitality that is bigger and deeper than domestic status, work, culture, and religious ritual. Until we are connected to the living water, we will keep coming up dry and empty, no matter what is in our family, cultural, or religious water pots and buckets.

God's love is the living water that Jesus spoke about to the Samaritan woman. We are designed to be nourished, invigorated, soothed, and cooled by the constantly flowing stream of God's love. We need the push of God's unstoppable love in the face of our setbacks. We need the comfort of God's healing love for our hurts and injuries. We need the assurance of God's always-flowing love as we deal with obstacles, disappointments, sorrows, and anxieties. You and I, like the Samaritan woman, need to be invigorated, soothed, and cooled by the flowing stream of God's love.

Here is the good news: **God's love comes to us!** Despite whatever situations, setbacks, disappointments, insults, conflicts, or frustrations life may present, God's love comes to us! The meaning of Jesus showing up in Samaria at Jacob's Well is that God's love shows up! Her marital history could not keep God's love from showing up in Jesus. The bigotry imposed on her people could not keep God's love from showing up in Jesus. The religious turf fight between preachers in her region and other preachers elsewhere about where people should worship could not prevent God's love from showing up in Jesus. God's love flows to wherever we are to call us, claim us, soothe us, invigorate us, renew us, and redirect us. We do not need to go to Jerusalem or elsewhere to experience God's love. Jesus at Jacob's Well, talking with a Samaritan woman, tells us that God's love comes to us, wherever we are, however we are, to fill our dry emptiness.

By the love that God has given us through Jesus, we are able to confront injustice. By that love, we draw strength to overcome adversity. By that love, we are called as instruments of peace in the face of conflict. Through that love, you and I are agents of hope to people in despair. As God has given us the living water of divine love in Jesus, God has made us part of that love with Jesus. Like a stream flows to fill dry places, God's love flows in Jesus to fill us and flows in those who are filled by that love to renew, reinvigorate, redirect, and soothe others. This is what happened to the woman of Samaria. God's love came to her. Eventually, she became part of that love to others in her community.

If pastors believe that God loves people in whatever aspect of life they present themselves, then we must proclaim that love from our pulpits. And our sermonic efforts should call and challenge people to trust God's love in their relationships with others without regard to ancestral, cultural, ritual, or other bases for treating people differently because of their sexuality.

New Millennium intentionally confronted our phobia and prejudice about sexuality by prayerful study. Rather than use Sunday school quarterly materials and lessons, New Millennium follows a book study approach. I try to prayerfully select books that would stretch us. We have studied writings by Howard Thurman (*Jesus and the*

Disinherited), Dan Southerland (*Transitioning: Leading Your Church through Change*), Rob Bell (*Velvet Elvis: Repainting the Christian Faith*), Daniel Vestal (*It's Time: A Journey Toward Missional Faithfulness*), and Samuel Proctor (*My Moral Odyssey*) between our formation in May 2009 and the fall of 2010—and many others since then. And during the fall of 2010 and the winter months of 2011, we studied a book that challenged us to prayerfully ponder the ethical implications of being Jesus-followers concerning the issue of human sexuality when we studied a book written by Jack P. Rogers (*Jesus, the Bible, and Homosexuality*).

Like it or not, people act out their beliefs and fears. The phobia about human sexuality has driven how many people think and act about sexuality—both for themselves and for other persons. But the Bible declares that "God has not given us a spirit of fear" (2 Timothy 1:7, NKJV). One of the most frequent commands found in our Scripture is "don't fear."

So our congregation prayerfully engaged in months of serious study and honest conversation about sexuality by following a study guide included with *Jesus, the Bible, and Homosexuality*. We watched videos that addressed how persons who are gay, lesbian, bisexual, or transgender are perceived and treated by religious people and the efforts of people who are gay, lesbian, bisexual, or transgender to find acceptance and affirmation as they try to live out their faith in God's grace and truth (*For the Bible Tells Me So* and *A Fish Out of Water*). Instead of adopting the usual fearful approach to human sexuality, we deliberately, prayerfully, and congregationally chose to study, listen, share, and trust the Holy Spirit.

I didn't introduce the sexuality study to make a political statement for the congregation or myself. As pastor, I introduced that study for the same reasons that guide whatever we study. Human sexuality is a reality that religious people, including followers of Jesus, cannot deny or avoid. Humans are sexual beings by design. But sexuality isn't a subject that religious thinkers have been comfortable engaging. Augustine, considered by some to have been the father figure of Christian theology, never seemed to be comfortable with the human body. More than a few people have expressed concern, if not regret, "that for many centuries the teaching of the Church on human sexuality has suffered from its adherence to Augustine's distorted emphasis."[3]

I led New Millennium to intentionally study and confront the religious phobia about human sexuality knowing that the study would challenge us. It did. One of our charter leaders eventually left the congregation because she didn't want to participate in it. She left with a clear conscience and remains in contact with us. Although others openly expressed anxieties, they committed themselves to the study because it marked the first time they were part of a congregation where human sexuality was being openly pondered, discussed, and embraced.

At the beginning of the New Millennium study of human sexuality, we agreed that our effort would be guided by some fundamental thoughts:

- Every person's opinion counts.
- Respect each other.
- Be open-minded and nonjudgmental.
- Have compassion.
- Maintain and protect confidentiality.
- Listen to each other respectfully.
- Disagree agreeably.
- Don't be afraid to grow.

New Millennium Church is a new church start. Most of our members are middle-aged and senior citizens. Most of us have been Baptists for decades. But regardless of our ages, varying levels of education, vocational diversity, racial diversity, and other factors, none of us had ever engaged in a serious study of human sexuality and Christian theology. Our study marked the first time we were able to openly discuss sexuality and faith. The study allowed us to follow the Holy Spirit as we listened to each other, as we read and pondered the assigned reading material, and as we intentionally met a gay couple who are followers of Jesus and whose domestic relationship has endured for more than forty years.[4] We were able to confront the truth that the Bible has often been misused to justify slavery, segregation, and subjugation of women. We studied principles of biblical interpretation. We prayed for one another.

Our study didn't weaken us. It gave us a new courage. We came to understand the importance of testing how Scripture is read and understood according to the life and teachings of Jesus Christ. Thanks to prayerful study, we were able to have honest conversations about sexuality and faith. We learned to celebrate the gift of sexuality with each other. We moved from fear to joy.

Our experience also allowed us to rethink and re-envision what covenant means. Covenant involves much more than a ceremony. Covenant is about commitment and relationship. Our study showed that heterosexuals enjoy economic, social, and legal benefits that are denied other people.

In our 2010 conversation with the same-sex couple who has been together for over forty years—longer than my wife and I have been married—we learned that one member of the couple was denied the opportunity to be in the other's hospital room overnight following a surgical procedure. Arkansas did not recognize their relationship, despite all its evidence of commitment, as legitimate. They could not marry. They could not file a joint tax return. They could not claim each other as dependents for healthcare benefits. For a brief time, they were legally banned from being adoptive or foster parents. No matter how committed they proved themselves to be to each other, their relationship was not considered legitimate. Meanwhile, people who are heterosexual were permitted to marry—and receive all the social, economic, and legal privileges associated with marital status—whether they were committed to each other or not.

As we became better informed about these and other aspects of heterosexual privilege, we remembered our personal and collective experiences with injustice. We recalled that marriage ceremonies did not protect slaves from being sold and separated from each other and that

Baptists misused the Bible to justify human trafficking, chattel slavery, and Jim Crow segregation. We recalled that black people and women were denied citizenship and social equality. We remembered the hurtful impact of those injustices.

Above all, we remembered the love of God as revealed in Jesus Christ. In Christ, those who were once considered spiritual outsiders—and outlaws—have been brought into a covenant relationship with God and one another. The relationship and commitment associated with it creates and defines the covenant. And at the heart of what that relationship with God in Christ means are the Great Commandments. We are called to love God with all of our being (including our sexuality) and love other persons as we hope to be loved. The essence of covenant is love and justice, not legality.

Months of prayerful study about faith and sexuality made us more aware of heterosexual privilege. We heard about and witnessed its consequences on people who have been branded moral and social misfits on account of their sexuality. We remembered Jesus, the embodiment of God's wonderful love, who embraced people who were considered moral and social misfits.

Through prayerful study, prophetic preaching, and worship that intentionally welcomes all persons in God's love, New Millennium Church no longer lives in fearful silence about sexuality. We rejoice in the diversity God has created, including the diversity of human sexuality. We rejoice that covenant is about relationship and commitment, not ceremony. And we affirm that the love of God we've come to know in Jesus calls us to be agents of love, truth, and justice. We aren't afraid of sexuality. We rejoice in it. We're inspired to be agents of God's love, truth, and justice concerning it in the true sense of covenant.

Prophetic followers of Jesus should give thanks, then, for the blessings of romance, sexual attraction, sexuality, and sensual desire. We should affirm that life includes the earthy sensuality and fragrances of spring flowers and the playful sounds of singing and chirping creatures. Let us affirm that humans are part of God's wonderful sensuous and passionate creation, and that we are to accept our sexuality, sensuality, erotic desire, and romantic yearnings as magnificent features of how God has fashioned us.

We should thank God for romance, sexual attraction, and the blessings people who are in love with and devoted to each other can know and enjoy. Let's teach young people that this is how God designed us. This is part of what God called "good" about us. Let's teach them how to accept and affirm that goodness responsibly, without using it selfishly or oppressively, and without being guilt-ridden about it.

There are love poems in our faith book because God has created us with the capacity to be committed and devoted lovers. God has blessed us with the capacity to experience sexual attraction and romance. God has created us to experience and celebrate the blessings of human sexuality, romance, and erotic desire as integral aspects of faith. We should live in the fullness of those gifts to God's glory.

And in the wake of the 2016 presidential result, prophetic followers of Jesus must challenge those who have shown themselves willing to hijack the meaning of "religious liberty" in order to justify bigotry and discrimination based on sexuality and gender identity. As a follower of Jesus, I will not be afraid to address that effort and its implications.

Discussion and Reflection Questions

1. When have you previously been part of a faith-based study about human sexuality?

2. What did you learn about human sexuality from your parents or other family elders? What did you learn from your past Sunday school groups, congregations, or other faith fellowships?

3. What have you been taught by pastors, Sunday school leaders, and other religious educators about the Song of Songs, sensuality, and erotic attraction?

4. How has your history concerning the above questions differed from that of other followers of Jesus you know and with whom you routinely interact?

Notes

1. This chapter is from a sermon that I delivered on August 30, 2015, at New Millennium Church. It is included, as revised, to challenge the notion that human sexual behavior must happen with a view toward procreation for it to please God. I have also added material from my 2012 presentation titled "From Fear, to Joy, to Covenant," delivered during the [Baptist] Conversation on Sexuality and Covenant held at First Baptist Church of Decatur, Georgia, and cosponsored by Mercer University and the Cooperative Baptist Fellowship. See https://vimeo.com/40774882.

2. See https://www.washingtonpost.com/politics/trumps-history-of-flippant-misogyny/2015/08/08/891f1bec-3de4-11e5-9c2d-ed991d848c48_story.html. An article that documents Mr. Trump's vulgar statement about groping the genitalia of women can be viewed at http://www.slate.com/blogs/the_slatest/2016/10/07/donald_trump_2005_tape_i_grab_women_by_the_pussy.html. An article reporting Trump's history of misogyny, including how he made unannounced appearances in dressing rooms of contestants in the beauty pageants he produced, can be read at http://www.vox.com/2016/10/8/13110734/donald-trump-leaked-audio-recording-billy-bush-sexism. None of Trump's behavior is countenanced in the Song of Songs, let alone validated.

3. Rod Garner, "The Thought of St. Augustine," found online at http://www.church-society.org/churchman/documents/Cman_104_4_Garner.pdf.

4. After the Arkansas constitutional and statutory bans on same-sex marriage were declared unconstitutional by my colleague, Judge Chris Piazza, in a courageous and well-reasoned decision issued on May 9, 2014, I had the honor to officiate the marriage of that couple in my court chambers on May 12, 2014.

CHAPTER 11

Religious Equality and the Gospel of Jesus
Circle, Collision, or Coexistence[1]

Just then a lawyer stood up to test Jesus. "Teacher," he said, "what must I do to inherit eternal life?" He said to him, "What is written in the law? What do you read there?" He answered, "You shall love the Lord your God with all your heart, and with all your soul, and with all your strength, and with all your mind; and your neighbor as yourself." And he said to him, "You have given the right answer; do this, and you will live." —Luke 10:25-28

In recent years a growing number of cities and counties across the United States have adopted nondiscrimination laws that cover conduct considered immoral by some persons, including reproductive freedom, sexual orientation, and gender identity, even if there is no comparable statewide law to that effect. According to the Human Rights Campaign, "As of January 28, 2016, at least 225 cities and counties prohibit employment discrimination on the basis of gender identity in employment ordinances that governed all public and private employers in those jurisdictions. This list does not include those cities and counties that prohibit discrimination on the basis of gender identity for city and county employees—such policies do not affect private employers in those jurisdictions."

According to the National Conference of State Legislatures, "five states—Alabama, Georgia, Mississippi, North Carolina, and Texas— do not have an accommodation law for nondisabled individuals. All states with a public accommodations law prohibit discrimination on the grounds of race, gender, ancestry, and religion. In addition, eighteen prohibit discrimination based on gender identity. Nineteen jurisdictions also prohibit age-based discrimination in areas of public accommodation."[2]

Litigants have brought suit based on such nondiscrimination laws concerning public accommodations, employment, and housing in various jurisdictions. To the consternation of some persons, courts have ruled in favor of parties who complained they were subjected to unlawful discrimination in public accommodations, employment, and housing based on the professed religious beliefs of defending parties, and despite claims by defending parties that their allegedly discriminatory conduct was motivated by sincerely held religious beliefs.

For instance, federal courts rejected the employment discrimination claim of a New Jersey nurse who alleged she was subjected to religious discrimination when she was fired from her job at a public hospital for refusing to participate in two emergency procedures, on religious grounds, that would have required termination of pregnancies.[3] In 2015 the Colorado Court of Appeals upheld a decision by the Colorado Civil Rights Commission that a cake shop unlawfully discriminated against a gay couple by refusing to sell them a wedding cake.[4] In 2013, the New Mexico Supreme Court held that a commercial photography business violated the state human rights act by refusing to photograph a same-sex commitment ceremony, and that the state religious freedom restoration statute did not protect the photographer from liability under the nondiscrimination statute.[5]

More states and localities have enacted nondiscrimination measures covering employment, public accommodations, and housing. More litigants have prevailed in discrimination lawsuits based on the non-discrimination statutes.

Burwell v. Hobby Lobby

On June 30, 2014, the Supreme Court of the United States issued, by a 5-4 vote margin, its decision in the case of *Burwell v. Hobby Lobby*,[6] in which the court, for the first time in its history, held that a closely held for-profit corporation has the right to claim religious belief in order to be covered by the federal Religious Freedom Restoration Act (RFRA).[7] The issue in *Burwell* was whether the contraceptive mandate adopted by the US Department of Health and Human Services under the Affordable Care Act violated RFRA. The Supreme Court held that the contraceptive mandate, although adopted to further the compelling governmental interest of guaranteeing cost-free access to contraceptive care, burdened the exercise of religion because it was not the least restrictive way to ensure access to contraceptive care.

This marked a major shift in RFRA jurisprudence. The Religious Freedom Restoration Act was enacted in 1993 by Congress after the Supreme Court ruled in *Employment Division v. Smith* that state unemployment benefits could be denied to two members of the Native American Church who were fired because they used peyote as part of their religious ceremonies in the face of an Oregon statute that made intentional possession of peyote a crime.[8] The statute did not include an affirmative defense for religious use. The unemployment benefits claims were denied because the firings were deemed "misconduct." After the denials were overturned on appeals to the Oregon Court of Appeals and Oregon Supreme Court on First Amendment grounds,[9] the US Supreme Court vacated and remanded the case to the Oregon Supreme Court to determine if sacramental use of illegal drugs violated Oregon's drug laws.[10] On remand, the Oregon Supreme Court held that Oregon law prohibited consumption of illegal drugs for religious purposes, but that the prohibition violated the free exercise of religion clause of the First Amendment.[11]

The state then took a second appeal to the US Supreme Court which upheld, by a 6-3 margin, the denial of the unemployment benefits by reasoning that because the Oregon drug laws were "neutral laws of general applicability," which did not target the Native Americans' religious practices, application of those laws to Native Americans did not offend the First Amendment. Justice Scalia's majority opinion emphasized that Oregon's ban on peyote possession applied to anyone who might possess peyote for whatever reason, and that the First Amendment does not allow a person to use a religious motive as justification for disobeying such neutral laws of general applicability. Justice Scalia cited an 1878 Supreme Court ruling which stated that "to permit this would be to make the professed doctrines of religious belief superior to the law of the land, and in effect to permit every citizen to become a law unto himself."[12] Thus, Justice Scalia wrote that generally applicable laws do not have to meet the strict scrutiny standard of review, which requires that governmental action that infringes on First Amendment liberties further a "compelling governmental interest" and be "the least restrictive" means for doing so.

Under the RFRA, when a neutral law of general applicability imposes a substantial burden on the exercise of religion, the validity of that law is reviewed under strict scrutiny (compelling governmental interest/least restrictive alternative) analysis. In the 1997 case titled *City of Boerne v. Flores*,[13] involving a dispute between the Archbishop of San Antonio and local zoning officials who denied a request to enlarge a 1923 mission-style church in an historic district, the Supreme Court held the RFRA unconstitutional when applied to the states under the Fourteenth Amendment. The archbishop successfully argued that his congregation had outgrown the existing structure so that the zoning decision denying permission to enlarge the structure was a substantial burden on free exercise of religion without a compelling state interest. The RFRA was later amended in 2000 by the Religious Land Use and Institutionalized Persons Act (RLUIPA), which statutorily redefined exercise of religion as any exercise of religion, "whether or not compelled by, or central to, a system of religious belief," and emphasized that the statute was to be "construed in favor of a broad protection of religious exercise, to the maximum extent permitted by the [statute] and the Constitution."[14]

The importance of the Supreme Court's decision in *Burwell v. Hobby Lobby* becomes more obvious when one takes this history into account. *Burwell v. Hobby Lobby* did not involve individuals who contended that governmental actions infringed on their freedom to practice their religious faith, as was the case of the Native Americans whose unemployment benefits claims were denied in *Employment Division v. Smith*. Nor did *Burwell v. Hobby Lobby* involve claims by a religious institution or entity, as was the case of the Catholic archdiocese in *City of Boerne v. Flores* that challenged a local zoning ordinance as a burden on the ability to exercise religion.

Burwell v. Hobby Lobby challenged a provision in the federal Affordable Care Act that health insurance cover "additional preventive care and screenings" for women, as specified in federal regulations which require coverage for "[a]ll Food and Drug Administration approved contraceptive methods, sterilization procedures, and patient education and counseling for all women with reproductive capacity." This mandate applies to all employers and educational institutions except for religious organizations. The regulations were controversial among certain religious groups, most notably evangelicals, Lutherans, and the Roman Catholic hierarchy, whose hospitals, charities, educational institutions of higher learning, as well as other enterprises, oppose contraception on doctrinal grounds.

The challenge asserted in *Burwell v. Hobby Lobby*, however, was not from a religious group, institution, or charity, but from a closely-held for-profit corporation, owned by evangelical Christians opposed to certain forms of contraception mandated for coverage under Affordable Care Act regulations. The owners of Hobby Lobby and Conestoga Wood Specialties, a furniture company owned by a Mennonite family, argued that the contraceptive coverage mandate was a substantial burden on the exercise of their religious liberty protected by the Religious Freedom Restoration Act.

The Supreme Court ruled by a 5-4 vote in *Burwell v. Hobby Lobby* that the contraceptive coverage mandate in the Affordable Care Act substantially burdens the exercise of religion. Writing for the majority, Justice Samuel Alito declared that "allowing Hobby Lobby, Conestoga, and Mardel to assert RFRA claims protects the religious liberty of the Greens and the Hahns [the family owners of those entities]," and rejected the government's contention that for-profit corporations could not be considered "persons" under the RFRA, noting that federal Health and Human Services regulations treat nonprofit corporations as "persons" within the meaning of the RFRA.[15]

State Religious Freedom Restoration Legislation

As the Supreme Court was considering the *Burwell v. Hobby Lobby* case and following its decision, state legislatures in several states debated bills aimed at creating state versions of the RFRA. In Arizona, the state legislature passed Senate Bill 1062, which was intended to amend an existing law and provide an exemption to any individual or legal entity from any state law if the law substantially burdened their exercise of religion, including Arizona law requiring public accommodations.[16] That measure was vetoed, however, by Arizona Governor Jan Brewer on February 26, 2014, after critics of Arizona Senate Bill 1062 observed that the measure would have permitted discrimination against anyone and was intended to target LGBTQ persons based on religious grounds.[17]

Arizona Bill 1062 was supported by groups considered politically conservative, such as the Center for Arizona Policy and the Alliance Defending Freedom. The Alliance Defending Freedom is one among a network of political groups funded by the National Christian Charitable Foundation, an entity supported by billionaire David Green, founder of Hobby Lobby.[18]

Bills similar to Arizona 1062 were introduced in several other state legislatures.[19] Most of those measures were defeated or withdrawn in the face of fierce opposition. But state legislatures in Indiana and Arkansas passed state versions of the RFRA introduced by proponents who contended that the measures merely protected the right to free exercise of religion as guaranteed by the First Amendment to the US Constitution. The Indiana Religious Freedom Restoration Act[20] (signed into law by then-governor and now Vice President Mike Pence) and the Arkansas Religious Freedom Restoration Act[21] (signed into law by Governor Asa Hutchinson) were supported by religious conservatives opposed to extending the reach of nondiscrimination laws to persons who are LGBTQ. Supporters of these measures and proposals similar to them have also expressed concern that antidiscrimination laws will force people with religious objections to same-sex relationships to offer services to same-sex couples or otherwise accommodate persons who are LGBTQ in ways that contradict their religious beliefs.

One of the interesting nonevents during the 2016 presidential campaign involved the way prophetic followers of Jesus, and even the Democratic Party candidates (Secretary Hillary Clinton and Senator Tim Kaine), appeared to ignore Mike Pence's public positions against equality for persons who are LGBTQ. When Donald Trump named Governor Pence as his running mate, prophetic followers of Jesus and the Democratic Party contenders for the presidency had abundant evidence about Pence's record.

As previously mentioned, Governor Pence signed the Indiana Religious Freedom Restoration Act into law only a year before he was selected as Donald Trump's running mate and has been a staunch opponent and leader in political resistance to LGBTQ equality for many years.[22] As a member of Congress from Indiana, Pence voted against passage of the Employment Non-Discrimination Act (ENDA), which would have outlawed employment discrimination based on sexual orientation and gender identity. He opposed repeal of the "Don't ask, Don't tell" policy that prohibited US military personnel from openly admitting or expressing they were gay or lesbian.[23]

Despite that history, Secretary Hillary Clinton and Senator Tim Kaine never mentioned Pence's opposition to LGBTQ equality during the presidential campaign. Senator Kaine did not even mention it during his nationally televised vice-presidential debate with Pence. One wonders whether prophetic followers of Jesus will remember the "love thy neighbor as thyself" mandate in Scripture now that Vice President Pence is in office.

LGBTQ persons are—like the robbed and beaten character mentioned by Jesus in the parable of the Good Samaritan (Luke 10:25-37) and the sick, starving, and ragged man named Lazarus whose plight was ignored by a wealthy man in another passage from Luke's Gospel (see Luke 16:19-31)—now desperate for evidence that prophetic followers of Jesus know and love God enough to see God in their plight. Given that prophetic followers of Jesus, like other evangelical religionists, have been strangely silent about Mr. Pence's record of opposition to LGBTQ equality, LGBTQ persons have reason to suspect that the same factors that have caused evangelical failure to understand and teach the Song of Songs may mean prophetic followers of Jesus will find ways to pass by "on the other side of the road" rather than obey the example of the Good Samaritan concerning their vulnerable social and political situation.

Obergefell v. Hodges and the Kim Davis Controversy

The various state RFRA measures and the decision in *Burwell v. Hobby Lobby* were followed by the June 26, 2015 landmark decision by the United States Supreme Court in *Obergefell v. Hodges*.[24] The Court held in *Obergefell* that state laws prohibiting same-sex marriage, including laws that refuse to recognize the validity of same-sex marriages solemnized in other states, violate the Due Process and Equal Protection provisions of the Fourteenth Amendment to the US Constitution.[25]

After the *Obergefell* decision, Kentucky Governor Steve Beshear issued a directive that county clerks begin issuing marriage licenses to same-sex couples.[26] When Kentucky Governor Steve Beshear ordered all state executive branch agencies to follow the decision in *Obergefell*, Rowan County Clerk Kimberly Davis requested that Governor Beshear issue an executive order that would exempt county clerks with moral objections from being required to issue marriage licenses to same-sex couples.

When Governor Beshear rejected her request, Kim Davis, who identifies as an Apostolic Christian in the Oneness Pentecostal tradition, began refusing to serve gay couples who sought marriage licenses from her county office. Then she refused to issue *any* marriage licenses, to same-sex as well as opposite-sex couples, based on her belief that by issuing licenses to same-sex couples she would be violating religious beliefs protected by the First Amendment.[27]

Four couples (two same-sex couples and two opposite-sex couples) brought suit against her in the United States District Court for the Eastern District of Kentucky.[28] They sought to enjoin Davis from enforcing her announced policy of refusing to issue marriage licenses to any couples based on her belief that by doing so she would avoid discriminating against same-sex couples. On August 12, 2015, US District Judge David Bunning issued a preliminary injunction that enjoined Davis "from applying her 'no marriage licenses' policy to future marriage license requests . . ."[29]

When both the Sixth Circuit and the US Supreme Court upheld Judge Bunning's order, Davis defied it by turning away several couples who sought marriage licenses based on her assertion that she was acting "under God's authority." Judge Bunning then held her in contempt of court and remanded her to jail until she complied with the court order to issue marriage licenses. She remained in jail five days and was then released after Judge Bunning ordered that she "not interfere in any way, directly or indirectly, with the efforts of her deputy clerks to issue marriage licenses to all legally eligible couples."[30]

Religious Liberty, Equality, and the Gospel of Jesus

The *Burwell v. Hobby Lobby* decision, legislative efforts to enact state versions of the federal Religious Freedom Restoration Act, the decision in *Obergefell v. Hodges*, and the Kimberly Davis controversy highlight the tension between the religious freedom guarantee in the First Amendment and the right to equal protection of the laws guaranteed by the Fourteenth Amendment. One suspects that the movement to enact state versions of the RFRA similar to Arizona Senate Bill 1062, Indiana Senate Bill 101, and Arkansas Senate Bill 975 will continue. Proponents of those measures have pointed to Kimberly Davis and contended that legislation is needed to provide a legal claim or defense to persons whose ability to exercise their religion is arguably burdened by governmental actions or regulations, particularly state and local nondiscrimination enactments that include sexual orientation and gender identity among the categories protected from discrimination.[31]

One can read the various opinions in *Burwell v. Hobby Lobby* and *Obergefell v. Hodges* to glean the divergent legal perspectives on the

RFRA, reproductive rights, and same-sex marriage. I am more concerned, as a follower of Jesus and jurist, with provoking serious thought and conversation about how the constitutional values of religious liberty and equal protection are understood vis-à-vis the "love thy neighbor" ethic in the gospel of Jesus.

How does the "love thy neighbor" ethos of Jesus square with respect for religious liberty and equality? How should followers of Jesus contemplate that ethic as we evaluate measures such as Arizona Senate Bill 1062, Indiana Senate Bill 101, and Arkansas Senate Bill 975?

These are not idle questions, nor are they only pertinent for judges, lawyers, legal scholars, and political officials to ponder. Whether one is religious or not, these questions force us to decide whether religious liberty, equality, and the love ethos of Jesus function in a circle, collide, or can somehow coexist. Because evangelical followers of Jesus are a significant part of American society, it is especially important that evangelical followers of Jesus and the people who lead, teach, and purport to represent them ponder these questions.

Another reason that evangelical followers of Jesus should ponder the relationship between religious liberty, equality, and the ethos of Jesus arises from reactions by political figures. Mike Huckabee (a former Arkansas governor, Fox Television personality, and former aspirant for the Republican nomination in the 2016 presidential primary) commented on Twitter that the *Obergefell v. Hodges* decision was a "flawed, failed decision" and "an out-of-control act of unconstitutional judicial tyranny."[32] Texas Attorney General Ken Paxton called the *Obergefell* decision a "lawless ruling" and pledged free legal defense for state workers who refuse to marry couples on religious grounds.[33] Chief Justice John Roberts and Justices Clarence Thomas and Samuel Alito each wrote separate dissenting opinions to the decision in *Obergefell* in which they criticized that decision as portending dire consequences for religious liberty. And as previously mentioned, Mike Pence, who, as a member of Congress, voted against a federal bill that would have outlawed employment discrimination based on sexual orientation and gender identity, is now the vice president of the United States.

When Kim Davis was held in contempt and jailed for defying Judge Bunning's court order to issue marriage licenses in obedience to the *Obergefell* decision, Governor Huckabee commented that her case illustrated what he called "criminalization of Christianity."[34] Huckabee organized a rally outside the jail where she had been held that was also attended by Senator Ted Cruz of Texas, another Republican presidential candidate, who said that Davis was a victim of what he termed "judicial tyranny."[35] Liberty Counsel, the law firm that defended Davis, issued a public statement that "Kim Davis is being treated as a criminal because she cannot violate her conscience."[36]

On the other hand, several other political leaders called on Kim Davis to comply with court orders. Former Florida governor Jeb Bush said that Davis "is sworn to uphold the law," while suggesting that some sort of accommodation be made for her.[37] Republican presidential candidates Carly Fiorina and Senator Lindsey Graham of South Carolina separately suggested that Davis should either comply with Judge Bunning's order to issue marriage licenses to all legally entitled couples or resign her office.[38] Former Democratic presidential candidate, secretary of state, and US senator from New York Hillary Clinton commented regarding the Kim Davis controversy that "officials should be held to their duty to uphold the law—end of story."[39] And to reiterate, Clinton, who enjoyed strong support from the Human Rights Campaign, failed to mention Mike Pence's long opposition to LGBTQ equality at any time after Pence was named Donald Trump's running mate.

Followers of Jesus know about and discuss the political arguments surrounding the decisions in *Burwell v. Hobby Lobby* and *Obergefell v. Hodges*, state RFRA legislative efforts, and the Kim Davis controversy. However, there is scant evidence that we are pondering them in light of the "love thy neighbor" ethos of Jesus. This seems especially true judging from the way white Christian nationalists—so-called "good evangelicals" and white national supremacists—overwhelmingly cast their votes for Donald Trump during the 2016 presidential election.

I have discovered no information showing that many evangelical congregations discuss religious liberty, equality, and the ethos of Jesus in our congregational Bible study groups. And I have scarce information that evangelical pastors often or consistently include references to the gospel of Jesus when they offer public comments about the relationship between religious liberty and equality.

I have heard and read numerous comments by religious people who are concerned that "conscience" or "religious beliefs" provisions should be enacted that exempt religious people from compliance with antidiscrimination laws that offend their genuinely held religious beliefs. However, I have yet to hear or read a comment from any of those concerned persons that cites the teachings and conduct of Jesus.

Religious Liberty and Social Justice as Gospel Imperatives

The Gospel accounts of the life and ministry of Jesus illustrate that he often violated religious laws and practices. Jesus healed a man who had been blind from birth on a Sabbath day (see John 9). He healed a man "covered with leprosy" by touching him, a violation of the longstanding religious view that touching a leper rendered a person unclean (see Luke 5:12-16). On another occasion, Jesus did not prevent his disciples from plucking heads of grain and eating them on the Sabbath (see Luke 6:1-5), cured a man with a withered hand on the Sabbath (see Luke 6:1-5), and posed this question to onlookers: "Is it lawful to do good or to do harm on the sabbath, to save life or to destroy it?" (Luke 6:9).

Jesus violated religious teachings and practices when he interrupted a funeral procession of a widow's only son, approached the bier where the dead man lay, and touched it before calling the young man back to life (see Luke 7:11-15). When Jesus healed a hemorrhaging woman and raised the dead daughter of a synagogue leader named Jairus by taking her hand and calling her back to life (see Matthew 9:18-26; Mark 5:21-43; Luke 8:40-56), Jesus violated longstanding religious tradition found in Leviticus and Numbers (see Leviticus 15:25-30; Numbers 19:11-13).

It is not remarkable when political pundits and people unfamiliar with the ministry of Jesus fail to analyze claims of devotion to religious teachings and beliefs by reflecting on the life and ministry of Jesus as they make pronouncements about religious liberty in the face of demands for equality from people who complain about oppressive practices and policies. However, when people who profess to be followers of Jesus do so in the face of these and numerous other Gospel accounts about Jesus doing things that violated religious traditions and practices, it is worth noticing.

At minimum, one would expect pastors, religious educators, and denominational leaders to ponder aloud how support for creating religious exemptions to public laws created to eliminate and discourage discrimination and protect people vulnerable to suffer from it squares with the example of Jesus. One would expect, at minimum, that people who profess to follow the New Testament Hebrew prophet, whose conduct so frequently offended traditional religious teachings and practices on behalf of vulnerable people that he was labeled a threat to public morality, would ask how and why it is consistent with the religion of Jesus to use religious beliefs and traditions as a license to discriminate against others who are vulnerable. Thus, I contend that failure to engage in such serious thought and discourse amounts to moral and ethical misfeasance, if not malpractice, on the part of evangelical followers of Jesus. In the same way, "good" white evangelical nationalists demonstrate a similar failure when they overlook and misunderstand the gospel mandate and remain derelict concerning racial inequality and racism.

During the 2015 session of the Arkansas state legislature, I addressed the Judiciary Committee of the Arkansas Senate to oppose a proposed RFRA measure that its proponent called a "Conscience Protection" bill.[40] I reminded the legislators that most white evangelicals staunchly defended slavery, racial segregation, and blatant race discrimination in education, employment, political activity, and public accommodations on religious grounds.

J. Daniel Hays has observed that "after the American Civil War, the 'curse of Ham' was used by white clergymen to fight the notion of racial equality and the rights that would accompany such equality (voting, education, etc.)" and that "the connection between this curse and the slavery of Africans continues to be taught to the church via commentaries that are reprinted and for sale even today."[41] In the same way that white evangelicals of my youth denounced integration and interracial marriages on religious grounds, Kim Davis and other evangelical followers of Jesus consider same-sex marriages, support for reproductive freedom, and other positions to be sinful.

Prophetic followers of Jesus should remember that white backlash against black aspirations for equality after the Civil War ended black social and political advances during the post-Civil-War Reconstruction period (1865–1876). These advances stopped after white supremacists extracted a pledge from Rutherford B. Hayes to remove federal troops who protected the recently emancipated African former slaves from terrorism, disenfranchisement, and discrimination in exchange for their support to make him president when the 1876 presidential election was decided by the House of Representatives. Twenty years later, in 1896, the Supreme Court of the United States placed a judicial stamp of approval on the American version of apartheid that came to be known as Jim Crow segregation when it decided the case of *Plessy v. Ferguson*.[42] The 1876 compromise choice of Rutherford B. Hayes to become president and the 1896 "separate but equal" Supreme Court decision in *Plessy v. Ferguson* pleased "good" evangelicals the same way 81 percent (four out of five) white evangelicals in the 2016 presidential election were pleased to elect Donald Trump and Mike Pence one year after the Supreme Court upheld the right of same-sex persons to marry in *Obergefell v. Hodges*.

We who believe in religious liberty must admit that, for many years, religious leaders justified sex discrimination by citing sacred passages that they argued show that women are inferior to men. We who believe in religious liberty cannot ignore the reality that some religious traditions continue to hold that interracial marriage violates Scripture and that Bob Jones University, the alma mater of Arkansas governor and former Drug Enforcement Agency director Asa Hutchinson, banned interracial dating until 2000.[43] Some religious systems continue to teach that it is morally wrong for women to exercise leadership over men. We cannot ethically evaluate the impact of state RFRA legislation like vetoed Arizona Senate Bill 1062 and enacted Indiana Senate Bill 101 and Arkansas Senate Bill 975 without remembering this history.

We must also recognize that current support among evangelicals for state RFRA legislation, aimed at using religious liberty as a shield against nondiscrimination policies and mandates, raises at least three unpleasant and unloving possibilities.

First, it suggests that evangelicals are unconcerned about the interplay of religious liberty, equality, and the religion of Jesus.

A second possibility is that demands for religious licenses, in order to avoid complying with laws enacted to respect the inherent dignity and entitlement to equality of each person, convey a message that evangelical followers of Jesus believe that their mistaken or outright fraudulent interpretation of religious liberty and fidelity outweigh the equality guarantee found in the Fourteenth Amendment *and* the love ethos we read about throughout the Gospel accounts of the life of Jesus.

Yet another (and equally unpleasant) inference—and one that strikes at the heart of my role as a state court jurist—is that state courts, which will have the first responsibility for adjudicating disputes arising from religious liberty defenses based on state RFRA enactments against nondiscrimination measures, will issue decisions that are adverse to persons oppressed by discrimination based on political timidity.

The third possibility is not to be taken lightly. As I wrote in another context almost two decades ago, "One need only read Taylor Branch's *Pillar of Fire*, the second part in his trilogy on the civil-rights era during the King years, and Juan Williams's *Thurgood Marshall: American Revolutionary* to realize that "although state court judges had the first opportunities to provide relief for civil rights violations, they almost never granted relief. What comes through is a picture of state court judges who were timid, unimaginative, and, in some instances, even disdainful of the arguments put forward by those who attacked racial segregation in our nation."[44] I contemplate state court decisions in state RFRA religious freedom and nondiscrimination measures controversies in the same light, and I am mindful that judges are elected by popular vote in thirty-nine states.

Respectfully, I contend that each of these possibilities is morally and ethically unacceptable. I wholeheartedly believe in religious liberty. Kim Davis must be free to practice her Apostolic Christian beliefs. She, like many others in our society, must be free to believe that marriage is a union between one man and one woman. But as a public official, Kim Davis is not free to make her deep and sincere beliefs the official practice of Rowan County, Kentucky. She can find authority for honoring the ideal of equality and justice not only in the Fourteenth Amendment guarantee of equal protection of the law. She can find authority for doing so also, and more fundamentally, in the life and ministry of Jesus.

I believe that devout photographers, bakers, hotel operators, restauranteurs, and other enterprising people must be free to believe and practice the tenets of their faiths, whatever they may be. They must be free to profess and proclaim what they believe to be moral, holy, and true. But that freedom does not operate in a sphere unto itself. It exists, and must be exercised alongside and in relationship with, the freedom of others to be protected from discrimination because of who they are, who they love, with whom they may be married or cohabiting, or what they may differently believe and how they practice those beliefs.

Simply put, in the same way that Jesus refused to use religious tradition as an excuse for disregarding suffering people, prophetic followers of Jesus must understand and affirm that religious liberty is no excuse for discrimination and other injustice. Devout people are not entitled to use religious devotion as a license for social, economic, and political bigotry and oppression.

This imperative arises not only from the fact that we live in a multicultural, pluralistic society that depends on each person tolerating those who are different. It is an imperative based on the commandment of Jesus that we who profess to love God must also love our neighbors as we love ourselves, including our neighbors whose beliefs, identities, relationships, and behaviors differ from our own and who are consequently vulnerable to physical, social, economic, and political oppression.

It is well past time for those of us who prophetically follow Jesus to say so and to act accordingly. Our LGBTQ sisters and brothers are, figuratively and practically, in a Jericho Road plight since November 8, 2016. They cannot afford for us to repeat the mistakes made by followers of Jesus after African Americans began asserting political, social, and economic rights during Reconstruction. Time will tell whether we who claim Jesus as Savior and Lord will allow the evils inflicted on former African slaves to be imposed on persons who are LGBTQ by people who claim to represent the radical, liberating, and inclusive love of God.

Discussion and Reflection Questions

1. How has your faith experience and religious education equipped you to be an advocate for equality and inclusion on behalf of persons who are lesbian, gay, bisexual, transgender, and queer? When have you witnessed discrimination and bigotry towards LGBTQ persons that was defended or rationalized on religious grounds, and how have you responded?

2. How do you reconcile discrimination and bigotry towards persons who are LGBTQ and the "love thy neighbor" commandment taught by Jesus?

3. Have your faith group, pastor, Bible study leader, or other religious educators offered opportunities for you and other followers of Jesus to dialogue openly and humbly about LGBTQ equality? If not, why?

4. What will you do now concerning LGBTQ equality after having read chapters 10 and 11?

Notes

1. The views contained in this chapter were originally presented on November 13, 2015 during a lecture bearing the same title that I delivered for the inaugural Baptist Joint Committee on Religious Liberty held at Fuller Theological Seminary in Pasadena, California. I am grateful to Brent Walker and Charles Watson of the Baptist Joint Committee for providing me the opportunity to think prophetically about an issue that I now believe was a leading factor in Donald Trump being supported by four out of five white evangelical conservative voters in the 2016 presidential election.

2. See State Public Accommodation Laws, www.ncsl.org/research/civil-and-criminal-justice/state-public-accommodation-laws.aspx, accessed January 10, 2017.

3. *Sheldon v. University of Medicine and Dentistry*, 223 F.3d 220 (3d Cir. 2001).

4. *Craig and Mullins v. Masterpiece Cakeshop, Inc., et al.*, Colorado Court of Appeals, 2015 COA 115 (August 13, 2015).

5. *Elane Photography v. Willock*, 309 P.3d 53 (N.M. 2013), *cert. denied*, 134 S. Ct. 1787 (2014).

6. *Burwell v. Hobby Lobby*, 573 U.S. __, 134 S. Ct. 2751, WL 2921709 (2014).

7. 42 U.S.C. § 2000bb et seq.

8. 494 U.S. 872, 110 S. Ct. 1595 (1990).

9. 75 Or. App. 764, 709 P.2d 246 (1985); *affirmed without remand*, 301 Ore. 209, 721 P.2d 445 (1986).

10. 485 U.S. 660 (1998).

11. 307 Ore. 68, 763 P.2d 146 (1988).

12. *Reynolds v. United States*, 98 U.S. 145 (1878).

13. 521 U.S. 507, 117 S. Ct. 2157 (1997).

14. 42 U.S.C. § 2000cc et seq.

15. Public Law 111–148 (enacted March 23, 2010), also known as Obamacare.

16. Arizona Senate Bill 1062, http://www.azleg.gov/legtext/51leg/2r/bills/sb1062s.htm.

17. See http://archive.azcentral.com/news/politics/articles/20140221brewer-religion-bill-1062-controversial.html, accessed January 10, 2017.

18. www.salon.com/2014/03/27/hobby_lobbys_secret_agenda_how_its_secretly_funding_a_vast_right_wing_movement/, accessed January 10, 2017.

19. Other states where bills similar to Arizona SB 1062 were introduced included Arkansas, Georgia, Hawaii, Indiana, Idaho, Kansas, Maine, Mississippi, Missouri, Nevada, North Carolina, North Dakota, Oklahoma, Ohio, Oregon, South Dakota, Tennessee, Utah, and West Virginia.

20. 2015 Bill Text IN S.B. 101, 2015 Bill Text IN S.B. 101.

21. 2015 Bill Text AR S.B. 975, 2015 Bill Text AR 975.

22. See www.theguardian.com/us-news/2016/oct/04/mike-pence-led-anti-lgbt-back-lash-trump. See also time.com/4406337/mike-pence-gay-rights-lgbt-religious-freedom/. Both accessed January 10, 2017.

23. See time.com/4406337/mike-pence-gay-rights-lgbt-religious-freedom/, accessed January 10, 2017.

24. *Obergefell v. Hodges*, 576 U.S. __, 135 S. Ct. 2584, 192 L. Ed. 2d 609, 2015 WL 2473451 (2015).

25. Constitution of the United States, Amendment XIV.

26. *Miller v. Davis* (E.D. KY. Civil Action No. 15-44-DLB).

27. Constitution of the United States, Amendment I.

28. *Miller v. Davis* (E.D. KY. Civil Action No. 15-44-DLB).

29. *Miller v. Davis*, supra, p. 28.

30. *Miller v. Davis*, 2015 U.S. Dist. LEXIS 105822 (E.D. Ky. Aug. 12, 2015).

31. The Arkansas Religious Freedom Restoration Act.

32. Anthony Zurcher (June 26, 2015), "U.S. Gay Marriage: Reaction to Ruling," BBC News.

33. "U.S. Gay Marriage: Texas Pushes Back against Ruling," BBC News (June 29, 2015).

34. Lee, Tony (September 7, 2015), "Mike Huckabee: We Must Stand with Kim Davis against 'Criminalization of Christianity,'" *Breitbart*.

35. Sneed, Tierney (September 3, 2015), "Ted Cruz: 'I Stand with Kim Davis,'" *Talking Points Memo*.

36. Liberty Counsel, "Kentucky Clerk Kim Davis Jailed for Her Conscience," September 3, 2015.

37. Gehrke, Joel, "Jeb Bush: Kim Davis Is 'Sworn to Uphold the Law,'" *National Review* (September 4, 2015).

38. Israel, Josh, "Only 2 Republican Candidates Think Kim Davis Needs to Quit or Follow Law," *Think Progress* (September 3, 2015).

39. Byrnes, Jesse, "Clinton: Officials Should 'Uphold the Law'" *The Hill* (September 3, 2015).

40. House Bill 1228.

41. J. Daniel Hays, *From Every People and Nation: A Biblical Theology of Race* (Downers Grove, IL: Apollos/InterVarsity Press, 2003), 53.

42. 163 U.S. 537 (1896).

43. See www.christianitytoday.com/ct/2000/marchweb-only/53.0.html, accessed January 10, 2017.

44. Wendell L. Griffen, "Judicial Accountability and Discipline," *Law and Contemporary Problems*, vol. 61, 1988, 75.

CHAPTER 12

Soulful Confessions of
People in Crisis[1]

God is our refuge and strength,
a very present help in trouble.
Therefore we will not fear, though the earth should change,
though the mountains shake in the heart of the sea;
though its waters roar and foam, though the mountains tremble
  with its tumult.
Selah. . . .
The LORD of hosts is with us;
the God of Jacob is our refuge. Selah. . . .
The LORD of hosts is with us;
the God of Jacob is our refuge. Selah
—Psalm 46:1-3,7,11

Think with me about acronyms—abbreviated words formed by taking the first letters of a longer phrase or title—such as USA (for United States of America), NATO (for North Atlantic Treaty Organization), and VIPS (Volunteers in Public Schools). The military routinely uses acronyms. Two acronyms commonly used by military tactical units—meaning units designed and organized for direct contact with opposing forces—are SITREP (the acronym for Situation Report) and SPOTREP (the acronym for Spot Report).

I served in the army, so my understanding of SITREP and SPOTREP comes from that experience. A SITREP is a report issued by a tactical unit to higher command about the status of the unit and its operational situation at twelve-hour intervals (0600 hours [6 a.m.] and 1800 hours

[6 p.m.] daily). A SPOTREP is a report issued by a unit to pass along information about an immediate tactical situation, such as contact with or observation of an opposing force.

You recognize the difference. The SITREP is a twice-daily report about a unit's operational situation and readiness. The SPOTREP provides information about an immediate change in the unit's tactical situation. Psalm 46 resembles a SITREP. The psalmist proclaims God to be a refuge (a place for shelter from danger) and strength (a protector, guardian, and champion against threatening forces). The psalmist uses words that describe a dangerous and fearsome environment: "Though the earth should change, though the mountains shake in the heart of the sea; though its [the sea] waters roar and foam, though the mountains tremble with its [the sea] tumult" (Psalm 46:2-3).

People who have experienced earthquakes and explosions and people who have been on boats or ships during violent storms know those are dangerous and fearsome situations. We do not associate shaking ground and rolling water with safety but with danger. When the earth starts moving and water is rolling, we need shelter. We need a safe harbor. We need to be someplace where the ground isn't moving beneath us and the water isn't boiling around us.

It is not unfair or inaccurate to describe our present situation as dangerously unsettling for many people. The environment is unsettling and unsteady. Distrust in political institutions was high before Donald Trump was elected on November 8, 2016 to become our next president. Mr. Trump's surprising victory has only made many people feel even more anxious.

Religious institutions and leaders were already considered untrustworthy before the 2016 presidential election season. The fact that 81 percent of evangelical Christians (meaning white Christians who self-identify as evangelicals) voted for Donald Trump is not likely to cause anxious people to seek soul shelter in evangelical congregations and faith communities that profess to represent God's grace, peace, and hope.

Distrust in business and commercial institutions and leaders was high before November 8, 2016. Voters elected a bombastic business tycoon known for using his wealth, fame, and white maleness as weapons against those who are not wealthy, not famous, not white, not male, not heterosexual, and not able to resort to violent means to achieve their goals. Who would trust a business climate led by someone like that?

And there is high distrust for civic leadership. People are reeling after seeing FBI Director James Comey use his stature as head of the nation's leading law enforcement and investigation agency to influence the outcome of the 2016 presidential election. They are shaken by news that operatives from Russia hacked into private email conversations of political campaign workers and leaked documents. They are disappointed and dismayed after learning from the leaked documents that leaders at the highest levels of the Democratic National Committee schemed to manipulate news reporters and commentators in order to harm Senator Bernie Sanders's effort to become the presidential nominee for the Democratic Party. At the local, state, and national levels, people do not feel good about civic leadership.

The day-to-day (SITREP) condition of people in our society and world is unstable, uncertain, and uneasy. From climate change to civic, social, religious, and other institutions, people feel afraid, anxious, angry, and alarmed.

And we seem to be constantly receiving SPOTREP updates that inform us of worsening conditions. A member of an elected school board in Blevins, Arkansas, posted a selfie of himself in blackface along with photos praising the Confederate flag and his personal firearms.[2] The mayor of Clay, West Virginia, and economic development director of Clay County, West Virginia, posted social-media statements comparing First Lady Michelle Obama to an ape.[3] White teenagers taunt Latino high school and college schoolmates. Women and girls are being berated, teased, and harassed.[4]

Meanwhile, the climate is made more threatening because of the defiant incivility of white male supremacists. White Christian nationalists and white male supremacists are having a field day celebrating how their forces not only contributed to the election of Donald Trump but also blocked President Obama's nomination of Judge Merrick Garland to the Supreme Court of the United States. Recall that not only did

Senate Majority Leader Mitch McConnell and Senate Judiciary Committee Chairman Chuck Grassley refuse to allow Judge Garland a confirmation hearing and vote, but that Senator John McCain publicly declared before the November 8 election that the Senate would not confirm a nominee if Hillary Clinton were elected president.[5]

Donald Trump's election has dismayed journalists, produced anxiety among US allies, and emboldened adversaries of the United States in Russia, China, Iran, and elsewhere. Hard-liner and imperialist leaders across the world are bolder, while people concerned about human rights, social justice, protection of the environment, and care of immigrants, poor people, homeless people, workers, the elderly, disabled, and other vulnerable people are troubled.

Honest faith admits these realities. Honest faith admits the uncertainty and anxiety triggered by these realities. Honest faith admits that the earth can and does quake, that mountains can and do tremble, that oceans do churn. Honest faith admits that we live in a world of real dangers, real threats, and real enemies to justice, peace, and generosity. Honest faith admits that we live in a world troubled by people who worship empire and greed. Honest faith admits that we live in a world made dangerous by purveyors of violence, fear, rage, hate, unbelief, and deceit.

Yet, we will not fear! We will not fear because we know God.

We will not fear because we know who God is.

We will not fear because we know God is our God, not mountains of politicians, not mountains of money, not mountains of political alliances, and not mountains of weapons.

God is *our* God.

God is *our refuge*, our hiding place, our shelter, and our covering in stormy and destabilizing forces and situations.

God is *our strength*, our Ally, Protector, Guardian, and Champion. *The* LORD *of hosts is with us.*

The God of Jacob (the cunning and thieving son of Isaac who refused to share his food with his hungry brother, Esau, but used his brother's hunger as an opportunity for selfish gain, and later schemed with his mother to trick his father into denying Esau the rights they knew he deserved), that

God who knows how wrong-headed we think and how wrong-hearted we are and how wrong-handed we act—that God is with us!

Instead of fear, we must look past Donald Trump to Jesus Christ! We should not look to the king of the American empire, but to the King of Calvary. Luke 23:33-43 places us at Calvary, not Trump Tower.

At Calvary, we are there, and so is Jesus.

At Calvary, our shortcomings and failings are on full display. So is Jesus.

At Calvary, we are ridiculed as defeated people, despondent people, marginalized people, and vilified people. So is Jesus.

The ridiculed Christ is with us.

The praying-for-enemies-anyhow Christ is with us.

The Christ who claims us when nothing looks hopeful is with us.

The Christ who claims us when we have no place to go is with us. That Christ is Jesus. That Christ is not Donald Trump. Jesus Christ is with us in this Calvary moment marked by the latest version of American greed, imperialism, racism, sexism, homophobia, xenophobia, materialism, militarism, and classism.

And Jesus Christ has a message for us. Jesus Christ says to us, each and all of us, "I tell you, today you will be with me in Paradise" (Luke 21:43). We have a place with Christ, today. We have a place with Christ, tomorrow. We have a place with Christ, always.

God is our help in Jesus Christ. God is our rock in Jesus Christ. God is our strength in Jesus Christ. We will not fear. We will not hide. We will not cringe.

We will shout hallelujah! We will believe in the Scriptures that proclaim:

> Great is the LORD and greatly to be praised. (1 Chronicles 16:25; Psalm 48:1; Psalm 96:4; Psalm 145:3)

> The LORD is my light and my salvation, whom shall I fear? The LORD is the strength of my life, of whom shall I be afraid? (Psalm 27:1-2, NKJV)

> In the time of trouble he shall hide me. (Psalm 27:5, NKJV)

The LORD is my shepherd, I shall not want. He makes me to lie down in green pastures; He leads me beside the still waters. He restores my soul; He leads me in the paths of righteousness for his name's sake. (Psalm 23:1-3, NKJV)

Yes! We walk through the valley of the shadow of death. Yet we will not fear! We choose not fear, but faith. We do not choose to flee forces of oppression but to face and fight evil however it shows up.

God's rod and staff protect us.

When enemies would cheat us, starve us, hound us, and lay siege on us, *the Lord* sets a table for us and will make our enemies supply the food and serve the table and then make them watch while we feast in safety.

Surely God is good! Surely God is able! Surely God is our help! Surely! Surely! Surely! Surely!

Hallelujah!

Discussion and Reflection Questions

1. What is your outlook concerning justice in the United States?

2. How has your outlook been affected by the election of Donald Trump as president of the United States?

3. How can you and other followers of Jesus, as advocates and agents of God's love, justice, mercy, and peace demonstrate the confidence reflected in Psalm 46?

Notes

1. This is a sermon I delivered on November 20, 2016 to the people of New Millennium Church.

2. See www.arktimes.com/ArkansasBlog/archives/2016/11/16/arkansas-school-board-member-photographed-in-black, accessed January 10, 2017.

3. See nytlive.nytimes.com/womenintheworld/2016/11/14/racist-facebook-post-about-michelle-obama-causes-outrage/, accessed January 10, 2017.

4. See abcnews.go.com/US/wireStory/schools-report-racially-charged-incidents-election-43476177, accessed January 10, 2017.

5. See www.npr.org/2016/10/17/498328520/sen-mccain-says-republicans-will-block-all-court-nominations-if-clinton-wins, accessed January 10, 2017.

Life after Election Day
The Fierce Urgency of Prophetic Citizenship

When the Son of Man comes in his glory, and all the angels with him, then he will sit on the throne of his glory. All the nations will be gathered before him, and he will separate people one from another as a shepherd separates the sheep from the goats, and he will put the sheep at his right hand and the goats at the left. . . . 41 Then he will say to those at his left hand, "You that are accursed, depart from me into the eternal fire prepared for the devil and his angels; for I was hungry and you gave me no food, I was thirsty and you gave me nothing to drink, I was a stranger and you did not welcome me, naked and you did not give me clothing, sick and in prison and you did not visit me." Then they also will answer, "Lord, when was it that we saw you hungry or thirsty or a stranger or naked or sick or in prison, and did not take care of you?" Then he will answer them, "Truly I tell you, just as you did not do it to one of the least of these, you did not do it to me." —Matthew 25:31-33,41-45

In every society and age, there are people who need shelter, food, and clean water; there are people who need healing from disease, illness, and injury; and there are people who have been locked out and kept away from opportunities not only because of mistakes and misconduct but also because they are targets of prejudice and bigotry. In every society and age, there are people who have left their homelands and need to be welcomed.

On November 8, 2016, 81 percent of the people who profess to be evangelical followers of Jesus in the United States refused to proclaim by their votes that God cares about people who are hungry, thirsty, homeless, frail, imprisoned, and unwelcomed. People who self-identified as evangelical Christians did not vote for, nor did they urge others to vote for, a candidate whose positions and records showed concern about people Jesus identified as God's surrogates in the world.

Hungry and thirsty people, homeless people, people who are frail due to age, illness, disabling infirmities, incarceration status or history, and immigration crises are God's surrogates. People marginalized due to religion, including people who are Muslim, are God's surrogates.

On Election Day, four out of five people who self-identify as "evangelical Christians" did not vote as people who understand, with Jesus, that hungry, thirsty, homeless, sick, imprisoned, and immigrant people are God's surrogates in the world. Their votes did not show that they see God in our hungry, thirsty, homeless, sick, imprisoned, and immigrant brothers and sisters.

So what can prophetic followers of Jesus do now?

We must practice *prophetic citizenship.*

Prophetic citizenship involves challenging politicians and our fellow citizens to focus on the needs of the people God cares most about. Prophetic citizenship forces politicians, the media, and our fellow citizens to see people who are hungry, thirsty, homeless, frail, imprisoned, and unwelcomed as the most important public-policy concern for every community.

Prophetic citizenship challenges politicians and the society-at-large—including people who say they love God and believe in God's love—to answer these and other hard questions:

■ Are public policies focused on the people Jesus mentioned in Matthew 25?

■ Are our tax dollars directed towards meeting the needs of the people Jesus mentioned in Matthew 25?

■ Are we holding President Trump and other officials accountable for serving the needs of the people Jesus mentioned in Matthew 25?

■ Are we who profess to believe in God's love for the whole creation and everyone in it making prophetic citizenship a priority in the way we live and how public policies work?

Lord, when did we see you. . . ?

Prophetic followers must insist that President Trump and his administration see God in our hungry, thirsty, homeless, sick, imprisoned, and immigrant brothers and sisters. We must constantly insist that the Trump administration recognize God in our vulnerable and marginalized neighbors.

Prophetic citizenship is not about building the American empire. It is about being what Howard Thurman called the Beloved Community. Prophetic citizenship recognizes, with Martin Luther King Jr., that the Jesus idea of love focuses on using power to achieve justice in a society, not greater profits for the affluent, not more weapons for war-making, and not more pain for those who are oppressed, vulnerable, frail, and alienated.

The last, and most radical, address that Dr. Martin Luther King Jr. made as president of the Southern Christian Leadership Conference (SCLC) was titled *Where Do We Go from Here?* Dr. King made this point quite clear in the following words:

> Now we've got to get this thing right. What is needed is a realization that power without love is reckless and abusive, and love without power is sentimental and anemic. Power at its best is love implementing the demands of justice, and justice at its best is power correcting everything that stands against love. And this is what we must see as we move on. What has happened is that we have had it wrong and confused in our . . . country.[1]

Prophetic citizenship produces public policies that implement the demands of justice. Therefore, prophetic followers of Jesus must now, with new urgency, challenge the administration of President Donald Trump to confront and address realities that he did not mention during the presidential campaign but that Dr. King and other prophetic followers of Jesus never allowed the politicians of their time to ignore or pretend to forget.

Dr. King insightfully and accurately characterized the state of social justice and civil rights in the last words we have from him in an essay titled "A Testament of Hope" that appeared in the January 1969 issue of *Playboy* magazine, of all places.

> Whenever I am asked my opinion of the current state of the civil rights movement, I am forced to pause; it is not easy to describe a crisis so profound that it has caused the most powerful nation in the world to stagger in confusion and bewilderment.[2]
>
> The problem is so tenacious because, despite its virtues and attributes, America is deeply racist and its democracy is flawed both economically and socially.

"A Testament of Hope" is the last and best evidence we have about how Dr. King saw and understood the plight of our society. Dr. King had the audacity to declare the unpleasant truth about the interrelationship of racism, classism, militarism, and materialism and the crippling effects of longstanding and studied indifference towards those evils. He did so as a follower of Jesus. He did so as a Baptist preacher and pastor. But most people have not read or hear of "A Testament of Hope". Instead, they go about trying to quote (and often misquote) segments of the "I Have a Dream" speech as if it were Dr. King's last will and testament.

Forty-seven years later, the evils Dr. King addressed so profoundly and prophetically have not been confronted.

Plainly, our challenge is to make Dr. King's vision work! We must quit genuflecting and making testimonials about the "I Have a Dream" speech and instead put our hearts and minds to work across racial, religious, income, regional, and other lines. We must speak and listen to uncomfortable truth. We must sacrifice together for the good of all.

Those who are privileged must use their power and influence to help those who suffer. We must shift our priorities from profits and property to people. We must become agents of radical change.

Becoming agents of radical change will begin when we quit talking about, reciting, and replaying the "I Have a Dream" speech as if it were the best thing Dr. King said. People who believe that repeating any dream over time will make it come true are either fools or insane.

We do not need more kum-ba-yah moments where we gather, hold hands, and sing "We Shall Overcome"—and then continue thinking and doing what we have always thought and done. Radical and systemic change requires radically different thinking and conduct from each of us. Those who resist that approach signal that they want things to remain as they are, no matter how much they quote Dr. King, sway while singing "We Shall Overcome," and talk about wanting things to get better.

Like Dr. King, I believe in hope.

Therefore, I reject the idea that we cannot be better than we are. But we will never be better if we maintain longstanding systems of inequality caused by the evils of racism, sexism (including homophobia), classism, militarism, imperialism, materialism, techno-centrism, and xenophobia. If Dr. King's vision of a just and peaceful society for all persons is to come true, we must put it to work as agents of radical change. Doing so will require that we recognize God, love God, and are pleased to be in kinship with God and the surrogates of God who are hungry, thirsty, homeless, frail, confined, and immigrants.

Lord, when did we see you . . . ?

We are followers of Jesus. Vulnerable people should find us standing to protect them from the oppression, neglect, and cruelty of the materialistic kingdom.

We are followers of Jesus. Needy people should find us standing among them and working to overturn the kingdoms that judge people based on how much they have.

We are followers of Jesus. People who are materially comfortable should find us insisting that those who've been blessed with more wealth are morally obligated to contribute more for the benefit of the common good. Yes, that will turn the anti-tax kingdom upside down. *We are followers of Jesus.* The lords of empire and war should find us turning over their kingdoms. How can we be followers of the One who said "blessed are the peacemakers" and somehow never be inspired to say no to war? How can we follow him who said "blessed are the merciful" and never insist on mercy rather than revenge?

We are followers of Jesus. Marginalized people should find us entering into authentic and loving community with them. They may be immigrants without documentation who are trying to provide for their families. Let us stand with them in the name of Jesus, who became an undocumented immigrant in Egypt. They may be marginalized because of their religion, or their sexual orientation, or their social history. The love of God revealed in Jesus impels us to cast off notions of privilege and enter into their experience.

We are followers of Jesus. So the disciples of the status quo will be offended when we shine the light of God's love in dark places and put the salt of God's truth to work on rotten realities.

Jesus said we will be unpopular, maligned, and persecuted if we live by God's love, but that when that happens we are to count ourselves with the blessed of God (Matthew 5:10-11). This is the reaction we must expect when we challenge the kingdoms of this world with the force of God's love.

I appeal to you in the name of Jesus to live for God in every breath and heartbeat as followers of Jesus Christ by the power of the Holy Spirit to turn the world upside down. Be agents of healing in a hurtful world. Be agents of welcome in a fearful world. Be agents of sacrificial generosity in a miserly world. In the name of Jesus, dare to live, love, suffer, serve, sacrifice, and even die to produce God's new order of love.

Then it will be said of us as it was of the sisters and brothers at Thessalonica: "These people who have been turning the world upside down have come here also, . . . They are all acting contrary to the decrees of the emperor, saying that there is another king named Jesus" (Acts 17:6-7). Amen!

Discussion and Reflection Questions

1. Consider these questions in your spirit: How can prophetic citizenship exist in people who do not live with prophetic hope? How can prophetic hope exist in people unwilling to see suffering people as surrogates of God? How can God be glorified when people who profess to know God refuse to see and treat suffering people as surrogates of God? What is the prophetic value of a notion of following Jesus that blinds itself to the surrogates of God and treats them as objects of derision, discrimination, exclusion, and punishment rather than divine calls to community?

2. What will you do as a follower of Jesus to "turn the world upside down" now that you have read this book?

Notes

1. Dr. King's last presidential address to the Southern Christian Leadership Conference, "Where Do We Go from Here?," is reproduced in *A Testament of Hope: The Essential Writings and Speeches of Martin Luther King, Jr.* James M. Washington, ed. (New York: HarperCollins, 1991), 247.

2. Ibid., 313.

Afterword

I anticipate that one of the key challenges we will have in these coming days is to hold fast to the need to bond pastoral reflection with prophetic action and prophetic reflection with pastoral action. We will be tempted to lean to one side or the other. This is the challenge we have always faced as people of faith seeking to live our faith in the world. We must remember that we are not called to take shelter in our faith in such a way that we remove our voices and our witness from the world around us. We are not called to be theological hermits or pious ostriches who refuse to engage our world with our faith and witness. No, we are called to live our faith out loud and with joy and celebration that we embrace the least of these, we open our doors for the strangers at our gates, we believe in the power of the empty tomb, and we live as Resurrection people who are not dead to life but deeply engaged in it.

This kind of faith infuses this book in ways that help us remember, through deep scriptural study and engaging reflection, that we have a pastoral and prophetic word to say to the nations—and to ourselves! Writing for prophetic followers of Jesus, Rev. Griffen offers us a clear-headed tough love that reminds us that rather than despair the results of our November 2016 elections, we must cast a stony eye to determine what we must do to be faithful to the religion of Jesus during the presidency of Donald Trump. This is no small question, given the ways in which faith has been twisted into an evil tree of rationalizations and platitudes such that Jesus would sanction hatred, misogyny, blind nationalism, and violence as the way in which we should engage one another. This book is a loud "NO!" to such blasphemy and instead encourages us to move forward with deep love . . . regardless.

We must face these tough times with fresh energy and urgency—and with a vigor that reminds us that we must stand on the frontlines of love. This is a love that is determined to face the challenges of our day, a love that is neither sentimental nor vapid, a love that is paired with justice such that, as black public intellectual Cornel West notes, love is what justice looks like in public. Our job as faithful folk is to build a more just society, and to do so, we need to harness the power of love over hate and violence.

As Rev. Griffen reminds us, we must stop being too meek and mild with our love, for love is not about being nice; love is not about being tolerant; love is not about our hormones running amok; love is not all emotion. *Love* is forged out of the biblical call to dig deep into our innards and find the spaces of compassion sequestered there, to pull them out into our social and political lives, and to create a society that values the great diversity of people that shapes us into a nation and helps us to be good global citizens.

This book troubles us, as it should. But it also shows us a way to live into our faith—relentlessly, in hope, and with eyes pointed to better days ahead if we work to make it so.

—Emilie M. Townes
E. Rhodes and Leona B. Carpenter
Professor of Womanist Ethics and Society
Vanderbilt University Divinity School

Rev. Dr. Emilie M. Townes, a distinguished scholar and leader in theological education, is dean of Vanderbilt Divinity School. In addition to being a pioneering scholar in womanist theology, her areas of expertise include Christian ethics, cultural theory and studies, postmodernism, and social postmodernism.